I0531775

Finding Beauty When
You Feel Broken

Even the Ashes Bloom

by

SARAH S. BROWN

©2026 by SARAH S. BROWN
Published by hope*books
2217 Matthews Township Pkwy
Suite D302
Matthews, NC 28105
www.hopebooks.com

hope*books is a division of hope*media

Printed in the United States of America

All rights reserved. Without limiting the rights under copyrights reserved above, no part of this publication may be scanned, uploaded, reproduced, distributed, or transmitted in any form or by any means whatsoever without express prior written permission from both the author and publisher of this book—except in the case of brief quotations embodied in critical articles and reviews.

Thank you for supporting the author's rights.

First paperback edition.
Paperback ISBN: 979-8-89185-404-8
Hardcover ISBN: 979-8-89185-346-1
Ebook ISBN: 979-8-89185-398-0
Library of Congress Number: 2025950941

Scripture quotations marked (NIV) are taken from the Holy Bible, New International Version®, NIV®. Copyright © 1973, 1978, 1984, 2011 by Biblica, Inc.™ Used by permission of Zondervan. All rights reserved worldwide. www.zondervan.comThe "NIV" and "New International Version" are trademarks registered in the United States Patent and Trademark Office by Biblica, Inc.™

Scripture quotations marked (ESV) are from The ESV® Bible (The Holy Bible, English Standard Version®), © 2001 by Crossway, a publishing ministry of Good News Publishers. Used by permission. All rights reserved.

Scripture quotations taken from the (NASB®) New American Standard Bible®, Copyright © 1960, 1971, 1977, 1995, 2020 by The Lockman Foundation. Used by permission. All rights reserved. lockman.org

Scripture quotations marked (NLT) are taken from the Holy Bible, New Living Translation, copyright ©1996, 2004, 2015 by Tyndale House Foundation. Used by permission of Tyndale House Publishers, Carol Stream, Illinois 60188. All rights reserved.

Sarah Brown's *Even the Ashes Bloom* is the kind of book that stops you in your tracks—not just because of the beauty of her words, but because of the deep, healing truth embedded within them. As someone who has spent more than two decades in publishing and helped launch more than 150 New York Times bestsellers, I don't say this lightly: Sarah is a voice we need right now.

Her writing is lyrical without being lofty, spiritually rich without being inaccessible. She weaves personal story with theological depth and practical reflection in a way that meets readers right where they are—in the ache, in the aftermath, in the valley. What Sarah offers isn't just insight. It's presence. It's hope.

Even the Ashes Bloom is an invitation to breathe again. To trust that beauty and brokenness can coexist. To believe that healing doesn't disqualify our faith—it reveals it. I believe wholeheartedly in this message, and in the woman behind it.

—Heather Adams
Founder & CEO, Choice Media & Communications
@heatherdixonadams

* * *

In *Even the Ashes Bloom*, Sarah shares her story of walking through the devastation of divorce with honesty and hope. But this book isn't just for those facing broken marriages—it's for anyone who has ever found themselves in a season of uncertainty, pain, or loss. Sarah weaves her personal journey together with biblical truth and practical application in a way that feels both tender and powerful. Her planting metaphor, brilliantly integrated throughout the chapters, beautifully reminds us that God is always at work—bringing life, growth, and unexpected blooms even from the tiniest seeds and the seemingly dead soil. This book is a gift of hope for the hurting and a gentle guide for those longing to see beauty bloom from their own ashes.

—Kristen Neighbarger
Author of *Breathing Again* & Author Coach

*　*　*

With courage and heartfelt vulnerability, Sarah shares her powerful journey from heartbreak and brokenness to a life beautifully restored by God's promises. Her story offers women a compelling path to hope and healing—reminding us that when we cling to God's truth, restoration is not only possible, but promised.

—Dr. Leigh Bagwell
Counselor, Author, Speaker

*　*　*

Vivid, raw, and redemptive, Sarah shares in her book—part memoir, part Bible study—with a voice that tenderly scatters seeds of hope. Using a powerful metaphor of ashes giving way to bloom, she shows how faith can take root, blossom, and bear fruit in the lives of others. With honesty and grace, she invites readers to step into their own story of renewal and discover the fullness of God's goodness.

—Stephanie Miller
Author, Speaker, Founder of Butterfly Beginnings Coaching
for Faith-Filled Writers and Creators

*　*　*

Like watching a master gardener tend scorched earth, Sarah's story reveals how God transforms our most painful seasons into fertile ground for unprecedented growth. The way she integrates personal narrative and biblical wisdom creates something both beautiful and necessary, reminding us that the bloom is worth the wait.

—Jennifer Burchill
Author of *Gifts of Gratitude: A Journey of Remembrance and Connection*

*   *   *

Honest and hope-filled, *Even the Ashes Bloom* reminds us that God calls us His beloved even in seasons of brokenness. Sarah Brown's relatable stories and practical BLOOM reflections make this a powerful companion for anyone walking through grief, betrayal, or loss.

—Tracy Harper
Bestselling author of *From Him, Not Them: A Young Woman's Guide to Relying on God for Validation, Identity, and Guidance*

For every woman who has ever sat among the ashes,
wondering if beauty could ever bloom again.
May you be surprised by the blooms God brings forth
in the places you thought were barren.

Acknowledgments

This book has been a labor of love. As it is about my life, numerous people have been a part of my story unfolding. Words of thanks seem like a small expression of gratitude in light of all the following people have done to help me discover the blooms among the ashes.

I am eternally grateful that God gifted me such beauty in my family. To my husband, Graham, thank you for making my dreams come true both as an author and for our family. Your words of wisdom, encouragement, and patience have carried me through the ups and downs of life. You are my always and forever, and it is an honor to do life with you. To my sons, Carter and Coleman, you are the lights and loves of my life. It is a gift to be your mother and have a front row seat to watch you become who God made you to be. May God always be your guide and hope. To my parents, thank you for your example in life, faith, and marriage. Your support and unconditional love mean the world to me. To Ross, Allyson, Braxton, and Adaline, thank you for welcoming Carter and me into your home when life took an unexpected turn. I don't know where we would be without your kindness, generosity, and love. To the Brown family, thank you for welcoming Carter and me with open arms and making us feel like we'd always been a part of the family.

God has blessed me with an incredible group of friends as well, who have listened to, laughed, cried, and prayed with me. To the Bat Girls, Leigh, Angeline, and Danielle, I will always have your back, and I have no doubt you have mine. I am grateful for the gift of your friendship, wisdom, and grace. When it was challenging to believe God had a good plan for me, Susan, Emily H., and Elizabeth, I am grateful you were there to lift me in prayer and help me find a place at work to hide and cry when it was all too much. To Emily E., Julie, and Melinda, I will be eternally grateful for our time together raising our boys, discussing life, and encouraging one another over chips and queso. To Ashley, Amy C., Charlotte, and my entire BGA family, thank you for being shoulders to cry on and friends to laugh with. You made coming to work each day a pure delight. To Amy W., I always look forward to our chats about life. Thank you for cheering me on as I wrote this book and as I take this step of faith. To Dawn B., I believe you are an angel on earth. Thank you for sharing your faith and beautiful spirit with me. You are the kind of woman of faith I hope to be. To Martha, thank you for helping me peel back the layers through therapy and always pointing me back to who God has created me to be. To Laura A., thank you for always offering emotional support and for helping me as I transitioned into single motherhood.

To Kristen Neighbarger, my writing coach, this book would not have come together without you. I am forever grateful that God made our paths cross when they did. These pages are filled with your influence, as you helped discover things I had overlooked and pushed me to clarify my message. To Amanda McMullen and Sara Davis, my editors, thank you for your expertise and insights, for asking questions, and for helping me grow as a writer. To my beta readers—Kristi P., Susan G., Monica J., Dayna K., Jenn B., Mary J., Susan J., Brianna B.—thank you for the gift of your time, honest feedback, and encouragement. To Brian J. Dixon, Hope Dover, and the team at hope*books, thank you for the opportunity to put these words in print and for your guidance along the way.

Above all, thank you, Lord, for your unending love, mercy, and grace. Thank you for your provision, presence, and peace. You are faithful to bring beauty from ashes. I pray this book brings you glory and helps others find hope.

Table of Contents

Introduction

"If God speaks to us at all in this world, if God speaks anywhere,
it is into our personal lives that he speaks."
—Frederick Buechner[1]

W e all have a story to tell. And perhaps one of my favorite things to do is hear the stories of others and listen for God's faithfulness throughout it all. The highs. The lows. The in-between. God is in our stories even when we can't see it for ourselves.

We live in a world that celebrates the highlight reel but struggles to hold space for the hard parts. But healing doesn't happen in the spotlight. It happens in the soul—buried deep, surrendered, and unseen.

This book is an offering from that place. An invitation to uncover what you've buried and trust that God meets you there. This is not a memoir, though I'll share my story. It's not a Bible study, though we'll open Scripture often. And it's not a step-by-step self-help manual, either. Think of this as a sacred companion—a guided journey through sorrow and surrender, with glimpses of hope along the way. Each chapter offers personal stories, biblical

---

1   Buechner, Frederick. *The Sacred Journey: A Memoir of Early Days*. HarperOne, 1982.

truth, and gentle prompts to help you reflect on your own path toward healing.

Frederich Buechner wisely wrote, "If God speaks to us at all in this world, if God speaks anywhere, it is into our personal lives that he speaks." I want to tell you my story in hopes you will see evidence of God not only in my life but that it will open your eyes to God's presence in your story as well, no matter where you are on the path from ashes to beauty. You don't have to be in a "good place" to begin this journey. You just have to be willing to look for God in the soil of your own story.

Biblically speaking, human life began in a garden, both literally, in Eden, and symbolically, in fellowship with God, rooted in relationship and purpose. According to the creation account in Genesis 2, God formed the first human, Adam, from the dust of the ground and placed him in the Garden of Eden: "Now the Lord God had planted a garden in the east, in Eden; and there he put the man he had formed" (Genesis 2:8, NIV).

Eve was later created from Adam's rib and also placed in the garden. The Garden of Eden was not just a physical location—it was a symbol of intimacy with God, provision, beauty, and purpose. It's where God walked with Adam and Eve and gave them their first responsibilities.

That image has deep theological weight, and it echoes again in Scripture, like when Jesus is found praying in the Garden of Gethsemane before His crucifixion—another powerful moment of surrender and redemption that happened in a garden.

And it makes me think maybe it's no coincidence that God meets people in gardens. In places of beauty, yes, but also in places of surrender, tension, and transformation. My own journey has unfolded in soil that felt dry and unworkable, full of disappointment and questions. And yet, that's exactly where I found God kneeling beside me—not rushing me toward healing, but tending gently to the broken ground.

I find it a bit ironic that God has used anything that grows to teach me more about who He is and the work He is doing in me. While the Garden of Eden was a lush, beautiful place, anyone who has seen my garden would describe it as quite the opposite. You see, I've never had a green thumb. You'll read more on this later, but suffice it to say that I recently bought a basil plant and couldn't even keep it alive long enough to make lasagna soup three days later. It's really that bad. My box garden would never be described as flourishing, since my lack of ability to sustain the life of a plant apparently extends there as well.

And yet, despite my love-hate relationship with tending the garden, it has been through dirt and dust, roots and fire, that God showed me something deeper: He's present in what breaks us and what rebuilds us. Our deepest brokenness can become the richest soil for growth when surrendered to Him.

This isn't just a book about pain. It's a book about hope.

The journey we are about to embark on together is one that will shine a light on places that we often prefer to stay hidden in the dark. Don't let that deter you from turning the page, because healing and hope are waiting for you.

Maybe you've come to this book with questions. Maybe you're carrying a loss no one sees, or wrestling with silent shame you've never named. Or maybe you're in a place of quiet hope, ready to believe again. Wherever you find yourself, I want you to know: your story matters. And God hasn't stopped writing it.

For me, the journey has been one from seeing myself through the lens of shame and failure, to seeing how God gently rewrites the story—not by covering the broken parts, but by stepping into them with me.

I'm a wife, a mom, a writer, and a woman who once thought she had to hide the broken parts of her story to be used by God. I've lived through loss, disappointment, and long seasons of silence. But I've also discovered God's presence in places I once tried to avoid. I don't have a seminary degree or a perfectly tended life, but I do have a story that's still unfolding, and a God who's been faithful through it all.

As you read each chapter, I'll share with you about my experience in the ashes of heartbreak and loss and what I have learned about God and healing in the process of facing it head-on. As we move through these chapters, I won't pretend healing is linear or easy. But I will testify to this:

The same God who allows the ground to break is the God who stays to water it.

Through stories, Scripture, and sacred reflection, we'll explore what it means to heal deeply, hope honestly, and bloom—even here.

We'll use the acronym BLOOM to end each chapter with action steps for reflection on and application of its contents:

- **B–Believe It:** The heart of the chapter—what I hope you'll take with you.

- **L–Linger:** Scripture to rest in and reflect on.

- **O–Observe**: Thoughtful journaling prompts.

- **O–Offer:** A simple, guided prayer.

- **M–Magnify:** A creative or symbolic action to deepen the message.

If you are one who struggles to journal, please do not let the journal prompts (*Observe*) feel overwhelming or like another item on your to-do list. Read the questions, think about them, and if you feel led, record your responses in a journal. I found journaling to be particularly healing as part of my processing the pain of the past. It has also been a beautiful reminder of God's faithfulness as I look back to see where I was then and where God has faithfully brought me to now.

I encourage you to approach the *Magnify* activity in the same way. Read through it, and if you feel led, complete the task. If you need to save it for another day, that's okay, too. There are no gold stars for answering every question and completing every activity; however, there is healing and hope to be gained.

Therefore, my prayer for you as you read this book is that you may acknowledge the places in your heart in need of healing and receive the restoration only God can provide.

God is in *every* part of your story—including the brokenness. He is present in the pain, mercifully guiding you toward hope and healing.

See, I am doing a new thing!
Now it springs up; do you not perceive it?
I am making a way in the wilderness and
streams in the wasteland.

(Isaiah 43:19, NIV)

May your eyes and heart be open to the presence and power of God at work in your life in this and every season.

I am thankful you are here.

1

Broken Ground
Bearing the Ache of Hidden Wounds

"How can we respond to the brokenness?
We have to dare to overcome our fear and become
familiar with it."
— Henri J.M. Nouwen[2]

The Breaking

The sunlight streamed through the living room window, warm and golden, the kind of summer day that usually made everything feel lighter. But not that day.

That day, everything shifted.

I had just dropped our toddler off at preschool and was supposed to have a movie date with my then-husband. He had the day off, and we'd planned to make the most of it. But when I

---

2   Nouwen, Henri J. M. *Life of the Beloved: Spiritual Living in a Secular World.* Crossroad Publishing, 1999.

walked into the living room, I saw him sitting on the couch, pale and afraid.

In a sudden panic, I asked, "What's wrong? What happened?"

He motioned for me to sit down beside him. That's when he said six words that cracked the world open beneath my feet.

"I've put our family in jeopardy."

I couldn't speak. I couldn't breathe. The words hung in the air like a dark, heavy cloud, blocking all light as they slowly crept into the cracks of my already broken heart. If it had been outside my body, my heart would have shattered into a million pieces right there on the floor.

I didn't need the details. Didn't need an explanation. I knew—he'd had an affair. In an instant, with six short words, everything changed.

The truth was, my marriage had been breaking long before those words were spoken. They just gave the fracture a voice. I felt like my whole world had come crashing down. The weight of a thousand dreams collapsing fell upon me.

As a young girl, I dreamed of being a wife and mom someday. At slumber parties, my friends and I would play M.A.S.H. (if you know you know), mapping out our fairy-tale futures: predicting who we would marry, what color our mansion would be, what car we would drive, everything right down to how many children we would have. It was quite a scientific approach, as you can imagine. Those giggly nights and the endless parade of baby dolls and imaginary play led me to create an idealistic vision of my future.

A loving husband. Two kids—one boy, one girl. A fluffy little dog. A white picket fence. Church on Sundays and weeknights at the ballfields. This was the kind of life I envisioned for myself.

To be honest, I thought I was building that dream. Until I wasn't.

"I've put our family in jeopardy."

The words sent my thoughts spiraling. It felt like the rug had been ripped out from beneath me. Almost instantly, I was a puddle of tears and a storm cloud of anger. I wanted to shake my fists at God and ask Him, "*Why?*"

How could a God who claims to love me allow for this to happen? How could He let such pain take root in my life? I had prayed for protection—for my husband, for our marriage, for our family. I believed those prayers mattered. I believed God was listening.

I remember sitting on the bathroom floor, back against the wall, tears streaming down my cheeks, barely able to breathe, as my heart tried to make sense of what had just happened. This wasn't just disappointment—it was devastation. I didn't just lose a relationship—I lost the version of myself that believed life would turn out a certain way.

Everything in my life felt broken.

In the days and weeks that followed, I went into survival mode. On the outside, I was holding it all together—working, parenting, managing life—but on the inside, I was quietly unraveling. My prayers became more desperate, more hushed. I didn't even know what to ask for anymore. I just wanted the pain to stop.

That's when shame crept in, slow and suffocating, like a fog. It clouded everything I believed about myself, my worth, and even God. I started asking questions I never thought I'd ask. *Was this my fault? Was I being punished for something in my past? Did I miss a warning God was trying to give me?*

It felt like the storm hadn't just hit my marriage—it had shaken the very foundation of my faith. And for the first time in a long time, I wasn't sure how to stand.

But here's the thing about breaking: it reveals what's underneath. Just like soil must be disturbed to prepare for new growth, something in me was being unearthed. There was so much happening beneath the surface—and even when I couldn't see it, God was at work in the mess.

I think back to a time when I tried to grow herbs in a small garden box in our backyard. Knowing next to nothing about gardening, I planted far too many seeds in a tight space. The soil became tangled with weeds, overgrown, and chaotic. Eventually, the landscaper came and cleared the whole thing out, cutting everything back to bare ground.

At first, I was frustrated. But looking at it now, I realize it needed to happen. The overgrowth had to be cleared. The soil had to be turned. And I had to wait. It took a full year before I replanted anything. But when I did, something new had space to grow.

My heart was no different. What looked like devastation was actually the beginning of a deep and holy excavation. God wasn't just cleaning up the surface. He was breaking the ground, turning the soil, and making space for healing to take root.

And like any soil that's long been untouched, what surfaced first wasn't beauty—it was buried pain. As God gently unearthed the layers, something long hidden began to rise to the surface: shame.

Wrestling with Brokenness and Shame

Shame had been growing beneath the surface for years—it didn't begin the day my marriage fell apart. In truth, it had already taken root long before I walked down the aisle.

I was twenty-one—young, idealistic, eager to follow God—but still unsure of who I truly was. As an insecure Christian woman, I stepped into a marriage covenant built on love... but also on shaky ground. Yes, we loved Jesus. Yes, we served in ministry—leading worship, praying over others, pointing people to hope. But love, even sincere love, doesn't always equal wholeness. And foundations, no matter how spiritual they look from the outside, can still crack under the weight of unresolved pain.

While we were dating, a piece of my past began to nag at me—a quiet ache I couldn't ignore. I knew if we were going to build a life together, he deserved to know the truth.

He had decided not to have sex until he was married.

I had not.

It was one decision. One relationship. A foolish choice driven more by insecurity than strength. Though I had confessed it and cried over it, begged God for forgiveness, and even believed He had given it—I still carried the weight like a scarlet letter on my soul.

Looking back now, I can almost imagine God bending close to say, "*Beloved, I already forgave you.*" But my heart wasn't ready to receive that truth because I hadn't yet forgiven myself.

I grew up in the era of True Love Waits—where entire youth groups stood on stages to pledge purity, and rings were given out like spiritual medals. While the movement may have helped some, for me—and for many others I have spoken with—it planted seeds of fear and shame. The movement talked about sex, but never about grace. It promised God's blessing for those who waited—but it didn't say much about those who hadn't.

For many of us, it planted a quiet message:
Sex is shameful. Desire is dangerous.
If you cross the line, you are damaged goods.

Sex was rarely talked about in healthy, hopeful ways. For some of us, it wasn't talked about at all. The conversation, if it even happened, was a one-time box to check. So instead of seeing intimacy as a sacred gift, I saw it as something that defined me negatively. And I wasn't alone in that. I've talked to so many women who still carry quiet shame about their past, never realizing God wasn't the one who gave it to them.

From the moment I became vulnerable in sharing out loud that I had not remained a virgin until marriage, I also opened myself up to the sting of rejection. Instead of grace, he measured my worth against my past. It broke me—heart, spirit, and soul— all cracked beneath the weight of trying to hold myself together.

One moment, in particular, shattered me. After we got engaged, my fiancé asked me to sit down with both him and my parents so I could tell them that I had not "saved myself for marriage," reasoning they "deserved to know *what* they were giving away."

Those words landed like a blow to the chest. I still remember the humiliation, the way my voice trembled, the ache that settled in my gut and stayed there for years. I didn't know it yet, but that moment marked a wound I would carry deep into my marriage— and far beyond it.

I was broken.

Not by my past. Not just by someone else's judgment.

But by the belief that maybe…maybe I really wasn't enough.

This was a question that haunted me long before I ever slipped on an engagement ring: *Am I really worthy of love? Will I ever be enough?*

I wrestled with this underlying seed of doubt and had come to believe that by having sex before marriage, I was, in fact, damaged goods. Fear crept in, telling me that no matter what I did, I would never measure up to my future husband's expectations, and a cycle of shame was set in motion in my heart and mind.

This kind of brokenness—left unspoken, unaddressed— begets more brokenness. When shame festers below the surface, it shapes how we see ourselves, how we relate to others, and what we believe we deserve. For me, the consequences were devastating: emotional abuse, a failed marriage, and years of spiraling thoughts I couldn't outrun.

God Speaks Truth Into Shame

Here's the truth about shame: it may be convincing, but it is not the voice of God. Shame speaks lies about your worth. God speaks truth about your identity. It took time for that truth to settle in.

At first, all I could hear were the echoes of guilt—but God's voice was there, even then. While I was silently questioning my worth, God wasn't standing off in the distance waiting for me to fix it all. He was near. Patient. Kind. He had already spoken forgiveness over me—I just didn't know how to receive it.

The journey from shame to healing didn't happen overnight. It started slowly, with small, steady whispers of truth—truth that began to break through the noise and reframe the way I saw God, and the way I saw myself. For a long time, I didn't know how to separate conviction from condemnation. I assumed the weight I carried was holy—that somehow, God *wanted* me to feel it. That maybe, if I felt bad enough for long enough, I could earn back His approval.

When my marriage began to fracture, I couldn't help but wonder if it was all connected.

Was this my punishment?

Was I reaping what I had sown?
Had God finally turned His back on me?

These are the kinds of questions shame whispers when you're already on your knees. But here's the truth I've come to know—one that I want to speak gently but clearly over you, if you're wrestling with the same questions:

God does not hold our past over us like a sentence waiting to be served.

He does not use heartbreak as a consequence for sin. He does not withhold healing or love as a form of discipline. Yes, God corrects—but always with kindness. Yes, He calls us to repentance—but not to shame. And yes, He is holy—but He is also wildly merciful.

In time, God began to unravel the lies I had wrapped around my identity.

I believed I was too much and not enough all at once.

But God called me chosen (John 15:16).

I believed my worth was tied to my past.

But God said I was made new (2 Corinthians 5:17).
I believed I had disqualified myself from His best.

But He reminded me that nothing—*nothing*—could separate me from His love (Romans 8:38–39).

As God's truth began to untangle the lies I'd believed for so long, something in me slowly started to shift. Not all at once—but enough to breathe again. Enough to hope again. And in that space, I began to wonder… *What if I could go back?* Not to change the story, but to speak kindness into it. To offer grace to the girl who didn't know she was already loved.

What I Would Tell My Younger Self

If I could go back and sit beside that twenty-one-year-old girl—the one carrying a ring and a secret, the one crying in her car after that conversation with her parents—I wouldn't tell her to toughen up. I wouldn't tell her to hide her heart better next time. I would tell her the truth:

> *God's not done with you.*
> *He's not disappointed in you.*
> *He's not looking away in disgust—He's drawing*
> *near with compassion.*
> *You are forgiven. You are loved. You are still worthy of joy.*

I would take her hand and say: This story isn't over. It's just beginning. And one day, you'll look back not only at the pain, but at the beauty God brought out of it.

Saying those words to my younger self brought a kind of healing I didn't know I needed. But even more than that, it reminded me of something deeper: God had been with me all along. Through every moment of shame, every tear-soaked prayer, every time I questioned my worth—He was there. Not just waiting for me to pull myself together, but sitting with me in the mess. That's the kind of God He is. The kind who doesn't wait on the other side of our healing, but meets us right in the middle of it.

God in the Broken Places

Every marriage begins with two broken people.

How do I know? Because "all have sinned and fall short of the glory of God" (Romans 3:23, NIV). No one enters a covenant perfectly whole. We all carry stories, scars, and soul-deep wounds.

Unfortunately, my brokenness collided with his.

And while his story isn't mine to tell, I can share how our pain played out. My wounds met his wounds. My shame met his silence. And instead of healing, we hurt each other in ways I couldn't have imagined.

One day, he said something I'll never forget. He told me that the reason he "put our family in jeopardy" was because I hadn't been a virgin when we got married. At the time, I was too stunned to respond. Looking back now, I see the red flag: the blame. The shifting of responsibility. Instead of owning his own choices, he pointed to my past and made it the reason for his. Hurt people hurt people. And in that moment, I was the one left holding the pieces.

Those six words—*I've put our family in jeopardy*—broke me all over again.

I was undone.

Shattered by circumstances I never saw coming. Crushed under the weight of betrayal, confusion, and grief that felt like it might never lift.

My marriage unraveled. My dreams imploded. And I was paralyzed—stuck in a cycle of fear, shame, and self-doubt. I didn't even recognize myself anymore. My heart was broken. And it felt like my hope was, too.

A silly little nursery rhyme came to mind one day, unexpectedly:

Humpty Dumpty sat on a wall;
Humpty Dumpty had a great fall.
All the king's horses and all the king's men
Couldn't put Humpty together again.

My heart, much like poor Humpty, had taken one heck of a fall. But here's the difference:

He was looking at the king's men. I had the King of the World.

And God? He wasn't trying to put me back together exactly as I had been. He was doing something deeper. Something redemptive. He was taking the broken pieces and making something beautiful.

Here's the truth I've come to know:

God does not leave us alone in our brokenness.

He's not afraid of our sorrow or our shattered places. He doesn't flinch at our wounds—He *runs toward them.*

Brokenness often feels like the end of the story. But with God, it's just the beginning. It's the soil where growth takes root. The place where we come face-to-face with our deep need and His deeper mercy.

We spend so much of our energy trying to hide the messiest parts of our stories—our anger, our grief, our doubts. But God isn't intimidated by any of it. He doesn't ask us to clean up before we come to Him. He simply invites us to come.

He invites us to bring it all. To lay it at His feet.

To trust that He can do something with even this.

God can handle your pain.

He welcomes your honesty.

He holds your sorrow and gently begins the work of healing—not by skipping past your brokenness, but by stepping right into it with you.

Your brokenness is sacred ground—not because it feels holy, but because **God is there.**

No One-Size-Fits-All Pain

My story may not mirror yours, detail for detail. Your wounds might look different. Your heartbreak may have come from a completely different direction. But pain is still pain—and brokenness, no matter the shape it takes, is always a place God is willing to meet us. That's why I want to pause here and acknowledge something important: **your story matters, too.** Your sorrow, your silence, your survival—they are not too small or too messy for God to care about. And there's no scale for suffering in the Kingdom of God. Every cracked and aching heart is held with the same tenderness.

In Henri Nouwen's book, *Life of the Beloved*, he describes brokenness in this way: "Our brokenness is always lived and experienced as highly personal, intimate and unique..."[3]

I want to honor your story.

Your heartbreak.

Your pain.

Your brokenness is personal and deeply unique, just as mine was. There's no comparing wounds. What fractured you may not have even registered on someone else's scale—but that doesn't mean it isn't real, or worthy of compassion and healing.

And while your story may be different from mine, here's what we both share: a God who is close to the brokenhearted. A Savior who redeems what feels beyond repair. A promise that **your pain is not the end of the story**. So what do we do in our brokenness? Nouwen encourages us to sit with it, writing:

> *How can we respond to the brokenness?...first befriending it and, second, placing it under the blessing... We have*

---

3   Nouwen, *Life of the Beloved*, 71.

to dare to overcome our fear and become familiar with it. Yes, we have to find the courage to embrace our own brokenness, to make our most feared enemy into a friend, and to claim it as an intimate companion. I am convinced that healing is often so difficult because we don't want to know the pain.[4]

If you're ready—even just a little—there's space to begin again. Space to sit with and embrace the brokenness. You don't need to rush past the ache or minimize what you've been through. Healing is a process, not a performance. And it starts by letting God meet you right where you are. He will meet you in the broken places—not to scold or shame, but to sit with you in them... and begin again.

What comes next is an invitation to rest in that truth. To slow down, lean in, and let God speak into the soil of your story—because even in this tender place, beauty is beginning to bloom.

Healing isn't a formula, but here's a simple way to walk with God through your broken ground:

---

4 Nouwen, *Life of the Beloved,* 75.

Beauty in BLOOM

B–Believe It
- God does not leave us alone in our brokenness. He meets us there with love, mercy, and healing.
- Your pain is not the end of the story.

L–Linger
- "The Lord is close to the brokenhearted and saves those who are crushed in spirit" (Psalm 34:18, NIV).

O–Observe
- In what areas of your life do you feel broken?
- How has your brokenness shaped the way you see yourself? What lies have you believed about your worth because of it?
- How has this impacted your relationship with God?
- Imagine Jesus is sitting next to you in your brokenness. What do you think He would say to you right now?

O–Offer Prayer
- Read Psalm 51:17 aloud. Pray, asking God to take this brokenness and use it for His glory.

M–Magnify
- Write a "But God" testimony.
- Finish this sentence in your journal:
- *"I was _____, but God _____. Now I know _____."* Even if you're still in the middle of your healing, take time to name one way God has shown up. This small act of faith magnifies His mercy in the mess.

2

In the Weeds

Questioning Who We Are
When Life Unravels

"Faith unchallenged is faith stifled."
— Beth Moore[5]

When the Garden Isn't What It Seems

For years, I stood on a stage next to my former husband and led others in worship. He was part-time staff at our church, and since I loved singing and music, I helped lead our weekly Sunday night worship service. During that time, I started serving in full-time children's ministry there as well. When he was offered a full-time position as a worship arts leader at another church about forty-five minutes from where we lived, I resigned, returned to teaching, and we moved to be closer to the community where we would be serving.

5   Moore, Beth. *Believing God Day by Day: Growing Your Faith All Year Long*, B&H Publishing Group, 2008.

The process for joining the church staff full-time and becoming an ordained minister included meeting with all of the church's leadership and elders. Much of this was done on his own, but at one point, I was asked to join my then-husband in the process.

The day of the meeting, I sat as the only woman at a massive table surrounded by men. Our pastors, most of the elders, worship staff, my then-husband, and I. I remember being asked questions about our marriage and what we, as a couple, would be contributing to the church and our community. I can still envision the moment I shared my desire to be a couple who served as mentors to younger couples in our congregation.

Only a couple of months later, my then-husband's affair started and would continue for two and a half years. When the day came that he told me about it, he also went to tell his boss at the church. I remember feeling gutted not only by the deception and infidelity, but also by the new layer of shame that fell like a blanket over my whole being. How was I supposed to show up for worship on Sunday and make eye contact with any of the staff who knew our marriage was falling apart? The elders who had heard me say I hoped we could serve as mentors to others? I felt like a fool. A complete, total fool. It was the most painful, embarrassing time of my life.

In the months that followed, I found myself questioning everything I thought I knew about people, community, and myself. Had I misjudged the places and people I thought were safe? It was like waking up in the middle of a lush garden only to realize that the beauty was camouflaging thorns. I didn't know whom I could trust. Every handshake, every Sunday smile, every "we're praying for you" felt suspect. Was it pity? Was it performance? Or had they always known more than they let on?

Maybe the hardest part wasn't just the external betrayal, but the internal invasion—the weeds that crept into my own heart. Shame, embarrassment, and guilt. All of it tangled together, choking out the parts of me that had once bloomed with joy and purpose. I had worked so hard to cultivate something beautiful—a marriage, a ministry, a life that looked fruitful from the outside. But the truth was, over time, weeds had begun to overgrow even my own soul. Pride. People-pleasing. A desperate need to be seen as "okay." And when everything came crashing down, I realized I hadn't just been trying to keep up appearances for others—I had been trying to convince myself, too.

What made it even more disorienting was how entangled the weeds had become with what once felt holy. Church was supposed to be a place of refuge, but now it felt like the scene of a crime. Every seat in the sanctuary and backstage hallway echoed with memories I didn't know how to reconcile. I would show up, force a smile, nod through conversations laced with spiritual niceties, but inside, I felt like my spirit was slowly being crushed under the weight of it all.

It wasn't just my trust in others that cracked. It was my trust in myself. The curated garden I'd worked so hard to maintain—one of faithfulness, leadership, steady obedience—suddenly felt like it had been overrun. I couldn't tell where my sincere offerings ended and my striving to be "enough" began. I was embarrassed to be seen and ashamed to be known. Every conversation felt like an exposure. Every glance was a reminder of the embarrassment and shame that I wore like a scarlet letter stitched to my soul. I questioned whether I belonged there and started shrinking back from relationships, unsure if people were offering help or just watching the wreckage unfold. I wasn't just grieving the loss of my marriage. I was mourning the death of who I thought I was.

God's Mercy in the Unfamiliar

If I asked you to draw a timeline of your life, you would likely start with a long, straight line. Then you'd mark it with important events from across the years of your life. The timeline of my life once seemed like that—one long, straight path. But if I drew it out for you today, you would see a space in the middle. There was a point at which everything became marked in my memory as either "before my world shattered" or "after that day."

It was in that "before" season, before I learned of my former husband's infidelity, that I signed up to serve on a mission trip to Rancho Sordo Mundo—a boarding school for deaf children tucked away in the broad valleys of Mexico. The trip wouldn't take place for several months, but the excitement built in me from the moment I heard about it. I enjoyed traveling, serving others, and have loved the beautiful language of signing since childhood.

My dad taught me some ASL, American Sign Language, when I was young. Not because anyone in our family was deaf, but because he had learned some sign language to communicate with deaf customers who came into his store, and he thought it would be fun to teach me, too. Though I knew no one who was deaf, I enjoyed being able to communicate with my dad at the dinner table secretly. Around Christmas or birthdays, we would tease my mom using sign language to communicate what presents we had picked out for her. She was unfamiliar with ASL, so I thought having this silent language between my dad and me was hilarious.

Over the years, I occasionally signed music in worship services and taught a small group at church what I knew of ASL. So, this mission trip was a chance to go abroad to teach about Jesus to children whose only language was sign, a language I had grown to love. Anticipation and excitement built as the mission team gathered to learn MSL, Mexican Sign Language, practicing common phrases and songs we could lead in worship while there.

Unbeknownst to me, however, the trip would fall in my life's "after that day" time frame. There was such emotional conflict within me as the trip approached. I was still excited for the opportunity, but the excitement was tempered by the mix of emotions I wrestled with since finding out about my then-husband's infidelity. It was like a tug of war within me—from excitement to anxiety, joy to sorrow. New worries bubbled up within me. *Will he miss me? Can I trust him while I'm away? Am I too emotionally and spiritually broken to be used by God?*

Looking back, I can see God's mercy written all over the decision to sign up for the trip to Rancho Sordo Mundo. He led me to that place *because* He knew what was coming. He knew that when the time to depart for the trip came, I would be in a much different place emotionally, mentally, and spiritually than when I signed up. He knew how much I would need the time and space away from what was familiar. God knew that the upheaval in my marriage made my home life feel unfamiliar, like uncharted territory, like dry, broken ground. In His mercy, He brought me to a physical place I didn't know, so He could lead me to a spiritual place of hope and restoration. What once felt secure had shifted, and the unknown became the path that led me to healing.

Silence That Speaks

I have always enjoyed listening to music or having some other soft noise in the background of my home. If it's the fall, you'll usually find my TV tuned to a football game, the soft roar of the crowd filling the quiet space around me. Other times, it's a playlist of favorite songs lilting from the speaker on my kitchen counter. So the irony is not lost on me; when the noise in my head and heart began to drown out truth, God led me to a place so quiet that even the people there didn't speak.

When we arrived at Rancho Sordo Mundo, exhaustion clung to me—not just from the long hours of travel but the long miles of heartache I'd already walked. Life felt heavy, uncertain. After the dust settled and the familiar stars blinked above us that first night, I opened my journal. I needed to put words to the ache inside me. I wrote:

> *"I am weary from the travel, and yet I am learning to trust my guide… God. I don't know what He will do in me this week, but I pray I'll be ready and willing to hear His voice."*

I didn't know it yet, but this would be a week of quiet stripping away—a time when God would start clearing the overgrowth I hadn't even realized was filling my heart.

We commonly hear the phrase *in the weeds* used to describe feeling overwhelmed, lost, or stuck in a difficult place. In day-to-day life, the "weeds" look like unanswered prayers, broken dreams, spiritual exhaustion, or relentless worry. Seasons of hardship, failure, and confusion can feel like wandering in the wilderness, being in the weeds. Feeling this way is not a flaw in your faith—it's part of the journey.

In the thick of it, when we feel overwhelmed by tough seasons, it's easy to lose sight of who we are. When life doesn't go according to plan—when relationships fracture, the dream crumbles, and the wait feels endless—we can question everything, including our worth. We start measuring ourselves by our circumstances and our failures. But the truth is: our identity isn't rooted in where we are or what we feel. It's rooted in Christ alone.

In the silence of those seasons, lies creep in: *You're failing. You're forgotten. You're too broken. You're not enough.* But those voices don't belong to God. They echo shame, not grace.

I've learned that seasons in the weeds are not just about external circumstances shifting—they're often about identity being sifted. In the wilderness, among the weeds, God peels back the labels we've collected from the world, others, and our inner critic. He removes what was never meant to define us and reminds us who we've been all along. Even in the weeds, we are still His beloved, still chosen, still redeemed.

Scripture is full of reminders of this truth:

"...you are mine" (Isaiah 43:1, NIV).

"Therefore, there is now no condemnation for those who are in Christ Jesus" (Romans 8:1, NIV).

"But you are a chosen people, a royal priesthood, a holy nation, God's special possession..." (1 Peter 2:9, NIV).

"So in Christ Jesus, you are all children of God through faith" (Galatians 3:26, NIV).

These are not just motivational phrases. They are who God, our Creator, says we are.

So if you're in the weeds right now, and you've started to believe that your worth depends on your productivity, relationship status, reputation, or ability to "bounce back," I invite you to pause. Ask yourself:

- What labels am I wearing that God never gave me?
- What truth about my identity in Christ have I lost sight of?
- What would it look like to live today as someone fully loved, even in the weeds?

When you focus on who God says you are, the noise begins to fade, and your heart reopens to the only Voice that truly matters. His voice always speaks love, purpose, and belonging—even when you feel lost, even when you feel undone.

As a perfectionist, I thought I had failed when I found myself in the weeds of broken dreams and unanswered prayers. But I have learned that God meets us most tenderly in the rough places. As Beth Moore shares in *Believing God Day by Day*, "Faith unchallenged is faith stifled."[6] Without the weeds, we could not truly appreciate and understand our need for God. Faith isn't static in the midst of them; it's stretched, shaped, and ultimately strengthened.

Sometimes, despite our most careful tending, weeds still spring up overnight. A sudden storm, an unexpected drought, or poor soil in one patch can throw everything off course. Life can feel that way, too—we do everything "right," follow the rules, pray the prayers, and put in the work, yet still find ourselves tangled in the weeds of heartache, confusion, or waiting. And no amount of "pulling them up" seems to fix it. But often, it's in those overgrown places that feel most forgotten where God is doing some of His most important work in us—not because we've failed, but because the outcome was never entirely in our control.

---

6   Moore, *Believing God Day by Day*, 212.

Some seasons call for perseverance, others for patience. Sometimes the wisest thing we can do is stop striving and simply ask, "Lord, what now?" But when we try to muscle our way through a hard season—thinking that pushing harder or praying louder will fix it—we often end up more tangled than before. God's way isn't about forcing our way out of the weeds; it's about trusting Him in them. Because in the end, tending a garden isn't about achieving perfection—it's about how we respond when storms roll in and weeds appear. And faith? It's not about avoiding the weeds altogether. It's about remembering who walks with you among them.

You may feel stuck in the weeds right now—a diagnosis you never expected, a relationship that's fallen apart, or dreams that have withered like parched soil. The weeds in our lives take many forms: toxic relationships, misplaced identity, insecurity, sin, idolatry, fear, shame, or loss. Whatever their shape, they have a way of distracting us from God. Even the strongest believers can lose their footing and find themselves in the weeds—a theme we see often in Scripture, where it's sometimes called the wilderness. The good news is that the wilderness is never wasted. These seasons have a way of exposing our fragility while revealing God's faithfulness.

Transformation in the Weeds

After months of wrestling with doubt, exhaustion, and a deep sense of being lost, I realized I had wandered into my own patch of weeds. I began to see that this wasn't only a season of suffering—it was also a place where distractions fell away and my true self was laid bare. In that stillness, God's voice grew clearer and more intimate.

God was using that season to refine me even while I was in crisis mode. Deep work was being done beneath the surface. The silence wasn't a void; it was an invitation. In the stillness, I began to notice the things I'd been too busy to see. The weeds—those tangled places I thought were in the way—became holy ground. They invited me to slow my pace, to sit with my questions, and to let God meet me in the uncertainty. I didn't need to figure it all out; I just needed to show up. Because sometimes, the most sacred growth happens not in our striving, but in our surrender.

We see the echoes of this in Scripture. Israel's journey through the desert revealed their fears, their dependencies, and their desperate need for God. They wandered, they wrestled, and yet they were never once forgotten. It shaped them for the promises ahead, just as it shapes us.

God's response to Israel wasn't driven by anger, as we often imagine, but sorrow. Even in their unfaithfulness, He refused to abandon them. Instead, He led them into the wilderness—not to punish, but to pursue. To strip away the idols they clung to, and to speak tenderly to their wounded, wandering hearts.

Hosea 2 marks the stunning turning point where judgment gives way to mercy, where abandonment is answered with an invitation, and where God promises not just to find His people, but to heal them—to replant hope in the soil of their shattered hearts:

> *Therefore, behold, I will allure her,*
> *and bring her into the wilderness,*
> *and speak tenderly to her.*
> *And there I will give her her vineyards*
> *and make the Valley of Achor a door of hope...*
> *I will betroth you to me forever... in righteousness and*
> *in justice,*
> *in steadfast love and in mercy.*

(Hosea 2:14–15, 19–20, ESV)

The beauty of Hosea 2 is not just in the poetry—it's in the promise. God doesn't just bring His people into the wilderness to scold them. He brings them there to restore them. And not to what they once were, but to something entirely new.

God Speaks Tenderly

Therefore, behold, I will allure her;
and bring her into the wilderness,
and speak tenderly to her.
(Hosea 2:14, ESV)

Before the vineyards grow and the doors of hope swing open, something happens first: God speaks. And not just any words, but words straight to the heart.

In Hebrew, "speak tenderly" literally means *speak to her heart.* As God speaks in the wilderness, His voice isn't harsh—it's healing. He is leading, not forsaking. He's inviting us closer, not pushing us away.

I know what it's like to feel stuck in the weeds, overcome by shame and past mistakes, wondering if restoration is possible. Maybe you know that feeling, too. But Hosea 2 makes it clear: God does not give up on us. He pursues us. He redirects us. He restores us. He draws us in and gives us hope.

Imagine God kneeling beside you in the weeds—not with a lecture, but with a whisper: *I see you. I'm not leaving you here. I'm growing something in you that you can't yet see.*

His tenderness isn't weakness—it's the fierce, covenant love that stays, that rebuilds, that refuses to walk away. When you quiet your heart, listen carefully: you might hear Him whispering to you even now, speaking not over your chaos, but straight into it.

Give Back the Vineyards

"And there I will give her her vineyards…"

(Hosea 2:15a, ESV).

God doesn't stop at tender words; He moves toward tender restoration. The imagery of vineyards is no accident. Vineyards symbolize abundance, fruitfulness, and stability—everything Israel had lost in her wandering. And yet, God says, *I will give it back.* Not because they earned it. Not because they finally got it right. But because He is gracious.

These may be the very things you might think are out of reach now. But restoration isn't just eventual—it's promised. God is already working, even if all you see today are thorns and brambles. It takes time to cultivate. It requires pruning, tending, and patience. This is the kind of restoration that doesn't just replace what was lost—it redefines it.

Trust that hidden underneath what looks barren, seeds are being planted. Roots are taking hold. A harvest is coming—one you can't yet imagine, but one that He has already prepared.

From Valley of Achor to Door of Hope

"…and make the Valley of Achor a door of hope"

(Hosea 2:15b, ESV).

And it gets even better: God doesn't just restore what's been lost. He transforms what once seemed irredeemable. The Valley of Achor, literally "Valley of Trouble," referred to in Joshua 7, was a place of sin, exposure, and consequence—a site of shame. But in Hosea 2, God flips the narrative.

Where there was trouble, He made a doorway.

Where there was despair, He planted hope.

The place of past failure becomes the place of future hope. Only God can do that.

Maybe your wilderness feels more like a dead end than a doorway. But in God's hands, even trouble becomes an opening. Even grief becomes a gateway to something new. He is always working, always redeeming, always turning broken places into beginning places.

Look closely. He doesn't say, *I'll take you around the valley.* He says, *I'll make it a doorway.* That wrecked place in your story? The one you don't want to talk about? The one you think disqualifies you? That may just be where God plans to turn into your personal door of hope.

Because in God's hands, your "too far" is never too far.

And if that weren't enough, He goes on to say: "And I will betroth you to me forever... in righteousness and justice, in steadfast love and mercy" (Hosea 2:19, ESV).

This is covenant language. It's God saying, *I'm not just healing you—I'm re-committing to you.* He's not keeping us at arm's length after our failures. He's drawing us closer, promising Himself to us with the kind of faithfulness only He can give.

So often, we come into the weeds like the Israelites were led into the wilderness, expecting punishment. But Hosea 2 shows us the truth: we are not being punished—we're being pursued. We're being wooed back into the arms of the One who never stopped loving us.

Just like Israel, sometimes we find ourselves feeling lost—doubting, broken, and struggling. Yet this isn't where God leaves us; it's where He lovingly leads us to healing and transformation.

Even in the wilderness, even among the weeds, God is working to restore us, offering a new identity and a fresh start.

Maybe you're standing in your own Valley of Achor, looking around at all that feels lost, broken beyond repair. If that's you, take heart: God's track record with wilderness wanderers is flawless. He never wastes a wilderness. He transforms it. Every single time. He doesn't just lead us out—He leads us through, shaping something in us that could never have been formed in easy places.

How to Walk Through the Weeds

When God leads us into quiet, tangled places, it's not to forsake us but to uproot the weeds of distraction and idolatry that keep us from Him. So, how do we walk through the weeds when we feel stuck?

- Recognize the Wilderness: It's okay to admit you're there. Honesty is the first step toward hope. Admitting you're in the wilderness doesn't drive God away—it draws Him near.
  - Rooted in Truth: "The Lord is close to the brokenhearted and saves those who are crushed in spirit" (Psalm 34:18, NIV).

- Listen for His Tender Voice: Instead of asking, *"How do I get out of here?"* ask, *"God, what are You speaking to my heart here?"* We practice tuning our hearts to the Shepherd's voice.
  - Rooted in Truth: "My sheep listen to my voice; I know them, and they follow me" (John 10:27, NIV).

- Trust the Vineyard Promise: You may not see fruitfulness yet, but God's promise is restoration. Faith looks forward to the vineyards even when all you see are weeds. Though the vineyard may seem slow to appear, God's vision will surely be fulfilled.

- Rooted in Truth: "For still the vision awaits its appointed time; it hastens to the end—it will not lie. If it seems slow, wait for it; it will surely come; it will not delay" (Habakkuk 2:3, ESV).

- Linger in the Wilderness: Linger in the wilderness without fear, remembering God is faithful. Brokenness doesn't have the final say—God's love and grace do. Even in long wilderness seasons, His mercies are new every morning.

  - Rooted in Truth: "The steadfast love of the Lord never ceases; his mercies never come to an end; they are new every morning; great is your faithfulness" (Lamentations 3:22–23, ESV).

Sometimes life feels like standing in the middle of an overgrown garden—surrounded by tangled weeds, wondering how on earth to get back to where you thought you should be. But just as a wise gardener knows when to prune, clear, and tend, and just as God tenderly led Israel through the wilderness, He is whispering to us now: *You're not stuck. You're not forgotten. You're being led.* Even when you can't see the rows taking shape, even when you can't yet glimpse the fruit, the God who speaks tenderly is already making a way. In His hands, what feels like trouble will one day become a door of hope—and beauty will bloom, even here.

Beauty in BLOOM

B–Believe It

- God uses the "weeds" to refine our identity, not to reject us.
- God leads us into quiet, tangled places to speak tenderly, restore what's been lost, and even transform our "Valleys of Trouble" into doors of hope.
- By listening for God's voice and trusting His promises, we position our hearts for the growth and restoration He is already working.

L–Linger

- Read Hosea 2:14–15. How does this passage encourage you about God's heart toward you, even in your struggles?

O–Observe

- Where do you feel "in the weeds" right now—spiritually, emotionally, or mentally?
- What lies or labels from your past are holding you back from embracing your identity in Christ?
- How has God brought hope from brokenness in your life before?
- What would it look like to surrender your "weeds" to God and trust Him with your healing?

O–Offer Prayer

Lord,

When I feel lost and weary,

Remind me that even the wilderness is not wasted in Your hands.

You meet me in the midst of confusion, in the silence of my questions,

And You speak tenderly, calling me back to life.
Where I see only pain, plant Your hope.
Where I feel forgotten, whisper that I am found.
Help me to believe that what feels like trouble
can become a door of hope—because You are the One leading
me through.
Root me in Your truth,
reshape my identity with Your Word,
and let beauty bloom even here,
in the weeds.
In Jesus' name, Amen.

M–Magnify

- Take a moment to cross out the lies in the chart below and rewrite the truths in your own words. Make them personal.
- Add to the chart past struggles or wrong beliefs you have carried. Then mark them out and replace them with truths from Scripture.

In Bloom Lie Vs. Truth

Past Struggle or Lie	Truth From Scripture
I'm too broken to be used by God.	"But He said to me, 'My grace is sufficient for you, for my power is made perfect in weakness'" (2 Corinthians 12:9, NIV).
God has abandoned me in this season.	"The Lord himself goes before you and will be with you; he will never leave you nor forsake you. Do not be afraid. Do not be discouraged" (Deuteronomy 31:8, NIV).
Nothing good can come from this pain.	"And we know that in all things God works for the good of those who love him, who have been called according to his purpose" (Romans 8:28, NIV).
I have to have it all figured out.	"Trust in the Lord with all your heart and lean not on your own understanding" (Proverbs 3:5, NIV).

Wherever you find yourself today—knee-deep in the weeds, waiting for hope to break through, or just learning to listen for God's whisper—remember this:

You are not lost.

You are not forgotten.

You are not beyond the reach of His restoring love.

The same God who speaks tenderly in the wilderness is still at work in you, even now.

Keep tending the ground of your heart.

Keep listening for His voice.

Keep trusting that even here, beauty can bloom.

3

Uprooted

Letting Go of What No Longer Serves You

"If you uproot an idol in your life and fail to plant the love of Christ in its place, the idol will grow back."
— Timothy Keller[7]

Joy in the Midst of Pain

The first few days of the trip to Rancho Sordo Mundo were spent doing various tasks around the boarding school's campus. Painting, doing laundry, and cooking meals for the children and staff. These simple tasks were reminders of home. Things I would be doing were I not in this place. With them came unexpected waves of emotion as I thought about all that awaited me when I returned home. My heart felt heavy as I sorted through emotions stemming

---

7   Keller, Timothy. *Counterfeit Gods: The Empty Promises of Money, Sex, and Power, and the Only Hope That Matters.* Penguin Books, 2011.

from the betrayal, embarrassment, and utter disbelief that my life had been so turned upside down.

Apparently, I hid the pain well. Josefina was the manager of the school's facilities and the wife of the director. She was deaf, but you could hear her heart through her expressive face and kind gestures. Early in the trip, she helped each member of my team come up with a way to sign our names. Rather than spelling them out letter by letter, Josefina took the first letter from our names and used it in a sign for a word she associated with us. Our group leader, Andy, was over six feet tall. So, naturally, she signed the letter *A* as part of the sign for *tree*. Thus, naming him "Tall Andy."

When it came time for her to assist with my name, Josefina looked at me with a smile and brightness in her eyes that I had never seen. I stood still, anticipating what word and sign she might associate with me. Despite the deep sorrow and wounds I carried with me, Josefina demonstrated the sign for *joy*, using the letter *S*, saying she could see the joy of the Lord within me. I tear up every time I think of that moment, still amazed that the joy of the Lord can break through even the darkest days. Unknowingly, Josefina had given me a dose of hope as she assigned my name. Hope that, though my soul felt crushed, God's Spirit within me, His mercy, His love, and His unending grace, were still far more powerful than any devastation I felt. So powerful that I radiated joy.

I carried that glimmer of joy into the days that followed, even as God began uncovering the deeper hurts I'd been holding back.

One morning, three of us women were assigned a simple but grueling task: clearing a dense patch of dry weeds near the students' dormitories. The risk of brushfires was real, and the brittle overgrowth had to go. We grabbed rakes and gloves and got to work.

The sun beat down as we raked and raked, pulling stubborn roots from the dust. And somewhere between the sweat and the aching muscles, conversations started unfolding between us— about life, heartbreak, and how tangled our hearts sometimes felt. As we talked, I finally reached a point where the pain of what I was going through poured out like a rushing river. I felt relieved to no longer hold it in and found comfort in being surrounded by women of faith who expressed no judgment, only a desire to pray with me as I began the difficult journey of processing my pain.

There in the dust and heat, knee-deep in stubborn thorns, God met me. I wrestled with some of the biggest questions I have ever asked God. I wanted clarity. I wanted a blueprint for my next steps, including whether or not I should remain married. I didn't realize it then, but I wasn't just wrestling with circumstances; I was wrestling with identity. Deep down, I was asking: *Who am I if my dreams fall apart? Who am I if my marriage ends? Who am I if I can't fix what's broken?* God's answer didn't come as a list of steps or fixes. It came as a quiet, tender whisper among the weeds: *You are loved. You are Mine.* God also offered me presence, silent, steady, enough. It wasn't the answer I thought I needed. But it was the foundation I didn't know I was missing.

As I dragged another armful of weeds into a growing pile, I realized that the work we were doing outside had become symbolic of the deeper work happening inside.

That night, still sore from the work of pulling weeds, I poured the day's lessons into my journal:

> *"God is our ultimate Gardener. He removes the weeds from our lives so that we can grow and flourish and become the beautiful, fruit-bearing people He's intended us to be. Just as we clear weeds to protect the children*

from fire, God clears out the sin and burdens that could consume us. As the weeds are pulled away, the ground takes on a new shape, ready for new growth."

It wasn't just the patch of ground near the dormitory being reshaped. It was my heart.

In the days that followed, as I worked among the weeds, pouring my heart out to those women, we wept, we laughed, we prayed, and we shared sacred moments in the presence of God. He met us there in the valley. This uncharted territory became holy ground as I learned to sit with the pain and pour my heart out before the Lord. All of it. The good. The bad. And the oh so ugly.

Weeks later, the weeds were gone, but their lesson lingered. I didn't expect it to resurface in such an ordinary setting—a Saturday at home, standing before my crowded closet. Yet as I began pulling things out, I felt the same nudge I'd heard in the dust and thorns: *It's time to clear the ground for new growth.*

At first, it was just a practical Saturday task—I had too many clothes I never wore, shoes that hadn't seen daylight in years, and a growing pile of "maybe someday" pieces that honestly weren't doing me any favors. Knowing they no longer fit, they may have even added to my insecurity. But as I started pulling things out, it became more than an exercise in tidying up. It turned into a spiritual excavation.

There was the dress I bought for an event I never went to—because I didn't feel confident enough to show up. The jeans I'd been saving for when I "got back to my goal weight." The shoes I kept because they looked good, even though they gave me blisters every time I wore them. Every item had a story. And some of those stories still carried grief—like the outfits tied to the relationship I had desperately tried to hold together. Every story revealed something I hadn't fully dealt with—striving, disappointment, fear of letting go.

But even in the ache of that moment, I sensed something beginning to shift. For the first time, I wasn't just organizing—I was listening. Letting the clutter speak. And in that listening, I could feel God gently nudging me to release what I didn't need to carry anymore.

Decluttering my closet became a moment of holy confrontation. God was inviting me to name the things I was still holding onto—not just in fabric and hangers, but in my heart. God was gently reminding me that new growth often begins with clearing what's been crowding the soil. While we all experience seasons where we're stuck in the weeds, we don't let the weeds completely take over our lives. There comes a time when we have to start pulling out those weeds, preparing for new growth. The same way we pull up weeds or prune dead branches, there are beliefs, patterns, and identities we have to uproot if we want to make room for healing.

This is the hard work of healing. The uncomfortable, grace-filled work of identifying what no longer serves our growth and letting it go, even if it once felt familiar or safe. Because sometimes, the most sacred work begins in the smallest, messiest places… like the bottom of a cluttered closet or a patch of weeds in the desert.

Recognizing the Root

I slid a new pair of running shoes out of their box and laced them up with determined optimism. *This time will be different*, I told myself, just like I had the last five times. Every few months, I'd launch into a new workout routine or healthy eating plan with enthusiasm. I'd stock the fridge with greens, set a 6:00 AM work-out alarm, and even announce my goals to my closest friends for accountability. Yet, without fail, two or three weeks later, I'd find those same sneakers gathering dust in the closet while I curled up on the couch, defeated by another abandoned plan.

It didn't make sense. In most areas of my life, I was high-performing and dependable. At work, I met deadlines and tackled projects with excellence. At church, I led a small group and never missed a meeting. Even at home, I kept our family calendar organized down to the last detail. I prided myself on being someone who followed through.

But when it came to my personal health—sticking to exercise or eating better—I felt utterly stuck. No matter how many Monday mornings I started with fresh resolve, by the end of the month, I'd inevitably slip back into old habits. It was frustrating, and if I'm honest, a little bit embarrassing. How could I be so disciplined in everything else, yet struggle so much in this one area?

I didn't have the answer yet, but I was beginning to realize this wasn't just about fitness. Something deeper was going on. Something I couldn't fix with a new planner or meal prep strategy. For the first time, I stopped blaming my willpower and started asking better questions.

One afternoon, over a cup of coffee, a close friend gently confronted me about it. She listened as I vented about my latest failed attempt at a new eating and exercise plan. Then she leaned in and asked softly, "Can I ask you something? You're so driven and reliable with work, showing up for people in need, helping others. Why do you think this area is so different? What's really holding you back here?"

Her question hung in the air between us. I opened my mouth to answer, but no words came. I honestly didn't know. I mumbled something about being busy or not *really* caring about having a supermodel figure, but we both knew I was dodging the heart of it. That night, her words kept echoing in my mind: *Why is this area so different?*

Over the next few weeks, that question refused to fade. I heard it when I hit snooze instead of getting up to work out. I heard it when I skipped breakfast and later raided the fridge, eating my cookies in guilty silence. *Why was this area so different? Why could I show up for everyone else, but not for myself?*

Eventually, I decided I needed help figuring out the answer. With a mix of reluctance and hope, I made an appointment with my therapist, who had guided me through some past challenges. If I could excel in so many parts of life yet keep stumbling here, maybe the issue was something deeper than just finding the proper diet or the perfect planner.

Sitting in my counselor's office a week later, I felt strangely nervous. I fidgeted with the hem of my shirt as I recounted my start-stop cycle with health kicks. She nodded thoughtfully and asked gentle questions: What did I feel each time I gave up on a plan? What was the narrative in my head when I skipped those workouts? At first, I offered surface answers—*I guess I'm just lazy… I get bored… I'm not disciplined enough.* But as she patiently peeled back the layers, I began to voice what was really going on beneath all those excuses. "I hate failing," I finally admitted quietly.

She gently offered, "There is a pattern here. It seems if you can't do something perfectly, you don't want to do it at all." It was as if a light bulb flickered on. In that softly lit room, with a tissue crumpled in my hand, I finally acknowledged the root of my struggle: perfectionism.

My therapist helped me understand that I had been sabotaging myself out of a fear of failure and a need for constant affirmation.

Not just in my health journey, but in other parts of my life, too—especially in the ways I had tried (and failed) to hold my marriage together through sheer effort. That familiar ache stirred again, and I began to understand how deeply this drive to perform and be "enough" had shaped so many areas of my life.

In every other arena of life, I knew I could meet the standards—often even exceed them—and I loved that feeling of accomplishment and approval. But when it came to my health, there was no immediate gold star or glowing performance review. The moment I missed a day or slipped up, I'd berate myself. To me, a single misstep meant the *entire* effort was a bust. The real issue was a perfectionist lie tangled around my heart, whispering, *If you can't do it perfectly, don't bother doing it at all. Better to not try than to try and fail.* That lie had put down roots in my life, especially in this area, and was choking out any chance of growth.

This revelation hit me hard and deep. I sat there, remembering all the times I'd given up and how each failure chipped away at my confidence. I had always thought my problem was just a lack of discipline or not finding the "right" program. But now I could see those were just surface issues—symptoms of something hidden underground.

My therapist didn't rush to fix it or offer a quick solution. Instead, she helped me sit with that realization and gently unpack its weight. In the sessions that followed, we worked together to recognize the patterns that fed this perfectionism. It wasn't just about the habits. It was about how deeply I had connected doing well with being worthy of love. She encouraged me to start small: name the thought when it came, interrupt it with truth, and remind myself that failure wasn't fatal. That I could be growing, even when I didn't feel successful. With her guidance, I began to see this wasn't just about breaking bad habits—it was about learning a new way to be kind to myself.

On the drive home from counseling, I felt a mix of relief and vulnerability. It was freeing to put a name to this pattern—perfectionism, fear of failure, whatever you want to call it. But I also knew naming it was just the beginning.

I whispered a prayer as I waited at a red light, asking God to help me. "*Lord, I need You to free me from this,*" I prayed, tears of earnestness in my eyes. "*I don't want to keep living in this cycle. Show me how to change—really change—this time.*" In my heart, I sensed a gentle assurance that I wasn't alone in this, and that God had been patiently waiting for me to invite Him into the struggle I'd kept in the shadows.

As I pulled into my driveway, I realized that what I needed most wasn't a better meal plan or a stricter schedule; it was a deeper healing. I had been so focused on treating the symptoms that I missed the root cause. It was like I'd been hacking at the leaves of a weed, frustrated that it kept growing back, when all along the root was still alive beneath the soil. If I truly wanted lasting change, I had to uproot the perfectionism and fear that had been quietly flourishing under the surface. And I knew I couldn't do that alone; I needed God, the master gardener of my soul, to help pull up those weeds.

That day marked a turning point. I wish I could tell you I woke up the next morning completely transformed and ran a mile without any fear of failure, but life change is rarely that instant or neat. Still, I did wake up with hope and a new perspective.

I decided to try a different approach: one small step at a time, lots of grace for myself, and an openness to let God work on my heart as much as on my habits. When I missed a workout or ate a cookie after dinner, I refused to call it a failure. Instead, I told myself it was okay to be human and kept going.

Little by little, those old all-or-nothing thoughts started to lose their grip. It felt like fresh air was blowing into a stuffy room in my soul. I was still working on building consistent, healthy habits, but now I understood that the real work was happening inside me.

Looking back, I can see that the issue was never really about exercise or diets at all—at least not in the way I thought. The true battle was with the unseen things: my craving for perfection, my fear of failing (and looking like a failure), and the lie that told me my worth was tied to my performance. Coming to terms with that was humbling, but it was also the beginning of healing. Because once I recognized the root, I could invite God to help me uproot it. And in His gentle way, He began to do just that.

As I share this story with you now, I do it with a smile and a much lighter heart. I'm still a work in progress—aren't we all?—but I'm not stuck in that same cycle anymore. By God's grace, the tangled roots of perfectionism and fear are loosening their hold. And with each bit of freedom I gain, I'm discovering that growth is finally taking place where I once felt barren.

Sometimes, the issues that keep us trapped aren't what they seem on the surface. Trying harder isn't the answer when the real issue lies beneath the surface. God invites us to let Him reveal and heal the root.

Before we dive into steps or solutions, we first need to pause and ask: What's really going on here? What unseen roots might be affecting the fruit (or lack of fruit) in our lives? It's not always an easy question, but it's worth exploring. After all, we can't heal what we don't acknowledge, and we can't uproot what we haven't identified. Our prayer may become the same as that of the psalmist David:

> *Search me, God, and know my heart;*
> *test me and know my anxious thoughts.*
> *See if there is any offensive way in me,*
> *and lead me in the way everlasting.*
> *(Psalm 139:23–24, NIV)*

We need to do a bit of digging, tenderly and honestly, to see what's hiding in the soil of our hearts. It might be uncomfortable sometimes, but remember, we're not doing this alone. The same God who lovingly showed me the root of my struggle is with us, ready to show each of us the things that need His healing touch. We all carry things that weigh us down, but we do not carry them alone. Even in our stuck places, God is with us. Some of these burdens in our hearts choke out joy and steal our peace; yet the Lord wants more for us, as those things keep us from fully growing into who He has called us to be. As we allow God to uproot unhealthy patterns—whether it's self-doubt, fear, lies we've believed, or even perfectionism—He makes room for new life to grow.

Once we've unearthed the root, what does it look like to begin pulling it out?

The Process of Uprooting

Uprooting is a *co-laboring* process. God doesn't force His way in. He invites us to partner with Him in surrender. And yes—it's often uncomfortable. Sometimes we need to let go of things we've carried for a long time. They've become like close companions on life's journey. But the longer we hold onto what's unhealthy, the longer we delay the growth God wants to bring.

Jesus Himself said, "Every plant that my heavenly Father has not planted will be pulled up by the roots" (Matthew 15:13, NIV). This verse reminds us that not everything growing in our lives is from God—some things may have taken root through fear, self-reliance, or the influence of others. Uprooting isn't just about discomfort; it's about discernment. It's the Spirit helping us recognize what was never meant to grow in us, and giving us the courage to clear space for something better. Only then can the soil of our hearts receive the kind of nourishment that leads to lasting growth.

So many times I have sat before the Lord with a tight grip on what I needed to release to Him. Not because I didn't trust God, but because I was unwilling to give up control. I told myself, "Shouldn't I be able to fix this myself?" And so, the uncertainty of the outcome and assertion of pride left me clinging to things that no longer served my healing. As I came to realize this, my posture of prayer shifted to one of open hands. Literally kneeling on the floor, palms open toward the sky, fully surrendering my mind, body, and spirit to God.

I came to know that surrender isn't about weakness.

It's about trusting the Gardener more than we trust the weeds we've grown comfortable with.

The work of uprooting can take shape in many ways: prayer, truth-telling, counseling, repentance, and community. We lay bare our wounds and weeds before God.

- **Prayer** opens the door to peace by giving God access to the parts we usually try to manage ourselves.
  - Rooted in Truth: "Do not be anxious about anything, but in everything by prayer and supplication with

thanksgiving let your requests be made known to God" (Philippians 4:6, ESV).

- **Truth-telling** is where freedom begins, especially the hard truths we speak out loud and stop hiding from. We don't have to fear the truth. When we bring it into the light, we make room for healing.
  - Rooted in Truth: "Then you will know the truth, and the truth will set you free" (John 8:32, NIV).

- God often uses **wise counsel**—therapists, mentors, spiritual directors—as part of His healing process.
  - Rooted in Truth: "Plans fail for lack of counsel, but with many advisers they succeed" (Proverbs 15:22, NIV).

- **Repentance** isn't just about confession—it's about realigning with God and receiving the refreshment He offers. Turning back always leads to grace.
  - Rooted in Truth: "Repent, then, and turn to God, so that your sins may be wiped out, that times of refreshing may come from the Lord" (Acts 3:19, NIV).

- Healing is often found in a safe, honest **community**—when we walk with others instead of hiding our hurts.
  - Rooted in Truth: "Therefore confess your sins to each other and pray for each other so that you may be healed" (James 5:16, NIV).

Which of these has God been prompting you to step into lately? What might He be inviting you to uproot so something new can grow? When we give more time and energy to the thing that is weighing us down rather than to growing in our relationship with Christ, we give more weight to the words of the world than the truth of who Christ says we are. Tim Keller put it this way, "If you uproot an idol in your life and fail to plant the love of Christ in its place, the idol will grow back."[8]

If you want to flourish, be willing to go there. Name it. Uproot it. Surrender it. Claim truth. And watch how the soil of your heart begins to make room for joy, peace, freedom, and the kind of growth that only comes through grace.

For me, pulling weeds meant more than just dealing with a broken marriage—it meant looking inward at my heart. I had to confront my own sin, my own insecurities, and pride. It was far easier to point at the pain caused by someone else than to acknowledge the ways I had fallen short. But without recognizing my own sin, I wouldn't have been able to see just how much grace I needed. We don't always want to admit that we play a role in our own struggles. But Scripture is clear: "If we say we have not sinned, we make Him a liar, and His word is not in us" (1 John 1:10, ESV). When we recognize our need for grace, we can better understand and extend it to others.

Patience is essential to the uprooting process. Deep-rooted struggles don't disappear overnight. And some weeds require persistent effort and the support of a community of fellow believers.

The Role of Community in Pulling Weeds

One day, I walked to the mailbox to find the dreaded letter from the HOA. *Great*, I thought, *what violation have we unknowingly made?* Sure enough, it was the weeds. The letter stated that the weeds in our front flower beds were visible from the street. We were instructed to remove them and mulch across the front of the house.

---

8   Keller, *Counterfeit Gods*, 172.

To be fair, they weren't wrong. I hadn't tended to the flower beds like I should have. Because life. Rather than being frustrated with the reprimand, I recognized the truth in their gentle nudging. The next day, I headed outside, trash bag in hand, to begin the back-breaking work of pulling weeds. With each pull, there was a certain amount of relief. I was one step closer to restoring the beds to beauty.

If I'm being honest, I can't say that I would have gotten the weeding done without the letter from the HOA. It just wasn't on my radar. I might have let them become much more overgrown had someone in my community not pushed me to uproot them, allowing for my other plants to flourish.

The truth is, we need community: people who help us face what we'd rather ignore, like a mirror that gently reflects the truth back to us. Dietrich Bonhoeffer writes, "The physical presence of other Christians is a source of incomparable joy and strength to the believer."[9] As we seek healing, accountability, and encouragement from fellow believers is an important part of the process. In our lowest moments, there is comfort in the presence of other believers. Likewise, they help us recognize where growth has stalled and walk with us as we rebuild what's been neglected.

God provided such a community on that mission trip to Mexico. Of the two women I sat knee-deep in the weeds with, one of them had also experienced a broken marriage. Her encouragement and words of wisdom helped me identify the very things I needed to uproot, as well as the beauty that remained scattered among the hurt. Amidst the pain, God granted me peace in the comfort

---

9   Bonhoeffer, Dietrich. *Life Together*. Translated by John W. Doberstein, HarperOne, 2009.

of community. He also used community to speak hope over me. Reflecting on that week of our time together, I wrote:

I have felt a sense of peace pour over me as I sat on my knees, face to the ground, praying with Amy. She prayed over me as I wept and let out all of the emotion that's been overwhelming me. As we cleaned out all the junk (weeds) from among the plants, we began to see the beauty in what was there but had been overlooked/ overgrown by the weeds.

God has given me beauty in the friendships I have formed here—especially with one of the other women here who has been through the same brokenness in her marriage as I have. God has provided me with such hope through her, her prayers, and her words of encouragement. I know that God can take our broken lives and make beauty from these ashes—He makes all things new and works all things together for the good of those who love him.

The community I experienced in this season didn't just help me pull the weeds; it helped prepare the soil of my heart for what God wanted to grow next. Their prayers, presence, and gentle truth-telling were like sunlight and water—essential ingredients in the slow, sacred work of restoration. Before anything can bloom, the ground has to be tended. And thanks to the people God placed around me, mine finally was.

After the clearing comes the planting. After surrender comes new life. The tender work God was doing in me—through truth-telling friends, tear-filled prayers, and those unexpected moments of grace—wasn't just about letting go. It was preparing me for a new season of growth. One I wasn't sure I was ready for… but one God had already made room for.

A New Season of Growth

As you know by now, I have a brown thumb. Like, impressively so. If thriving plants had a group chat, mine would send out SOS messages. But even I know this much: surface-level fixes only go so far.

The same is true for our hearts.

Temporary adjustments might make things look better on the outside. We try to "clean up" our attitudes or patch over our pain with busyness or positivity. But if we never address what's taking root underneath—fear, bitterness, shame, pride—then nothing truly changes. We find ourselves stuck in the same cycles, wondering why the struggle keeps resurfacing.

But when we invite God into the deeper work, He doesn't just tidy up what's visible. He renews what's beneath the surface. And here's the beautiful part: He doesn't leave that space barren. He prepares us for a new season—planting hope where weariness once lived.

Healing isn't only about what's removed—it's also about what takes root in its place.

I still hear that old perfectionist voice sometimes. But now, thanks to those counseling sessions, I recognize it for what it is—a weed God never planted. I've learned to pause, take a breath, and remember: growth isn't about getting it all right. It's about showing up, even when it's messy.

Growth begins not with striving, but with surrender. Not with our own strength, but with the Spirit's power. We don't grow because we try harder. We grow because we yield ourselves to the Master Gardener.

Paul wrote to the Corinthians, "So neither the one who plants nor the one who waters is anything, but only God, who makes things grow" (1 Corinthians 3:7, NIV). It's the Holy Spirit who brings transformation. Our job is to stay open, to be willing soil.

Sometimes growth looks like big breakthroughs. But often, it's small: choosing peace over control, forgiveness over resentment, or truth over old lies. It's learning to sit with God in the silence, trusting that even if we can't see the fruit yet, something is happening beneath the surface.

Because it always starts there, underground, unseen.

Beauty in BLOOM

B–Believe It

- God calls us to recognize and uproot the unhealthy things in our lives, even when it is painful, so that new growth can occur.

L–Linger

- "Every plant that my heavenly Father has not planted will be pulled up by the roots" (Matthew 15:13, NIV).

O–Observe

- Take a moment to sit quietly with God and ask: *Lord, what in my life have I allowed to grow that You never planted?*
- What feels hard to let go of?
- What might be taking up space in your heart that God wants to clear out to make room for something better? What has been keeping you from fully experiencing His grace and healing?
- Who in your life can walk alongside you in this process?

O–Offer Prayer

God,

You see the things in me that are holding me back—old wounds, fears, and patterns I've carried for too long.

I don't want to stay stuck.

Even when letting go feels hard, help me trust that You're leading me toward healing.

Give me the strength to release what's not from You.

Fill those empty spaces with Your truth and grace.

Soften my heart to Your presence and open my eyes to the people You've placed around me to walk with me.

Thank You for being patient, for not giving up on me,

and for always making room for something new to grow.

In Jesus' name, Amen.

M–Magnify

- Physically pull a few weeds from the ground, reflecting on the difficulty of removing them and what they symbolize in your life.
- When weeds are pulled, something new may be planted in their place. Visit a local nursery and choose something beautiful to plant in the place where you removed the weeds. Let this serve as a reminder of the work God is doing in your heart.

4

The Burn Pile

Releasing the Past and Trusting the God Who Restores

"Of one thing I am perfectly sure: God's story never ends with ashes." — Elizabeth Elliott[10]

The Burn Pile: A Holy Surrender

I stood upon the now bare patch of land that once held the overgrowth of weeds. It was dusty, dry, and appeared lifeless. Oswaldo, a former student turned employee at the ranch, pulled up in his rusty, silver pickup truck. He had hauled off multiple loads of the brush we had removed from the ground.

This time, however, as he went to start the truck, with the tailgate still open, he asked the three of us who had spent days among the weeds if we wanted to join him to burn all of the brush. This may have seemed an odd request to most, but all three of us replied with an enthusiastic, "Yes, please!" We quickly hopped on

10   Elliot, Elisabeth. *These Strange Ashes: Is God Still in Charge?* Revell, 2004.

the tailgate, feet dangling, and slowly rode across the valley to a part of the property where materials could be safely burned, far away from the school's buildings.

Watching as Oswaldo tossed the first match onto the pile was thrilling. Although he was deaf and could not hear us, he communicated with his facial expressions and hands. Seeing his reaction to us watching the weeds burn and understanding why this was such an emotional moment for us was simply beautiful. But the most beautiful part of that moment was the intense heat of the flames and the billowing smoke. It was a visual reminder of the work God had done in our hearts that week. While we couldn't see the beauty that would come from the brokenness we each felt, we could trust the God who held us close in those moments to bring restoration and hope. The ashes were not the end of the story.

As the flames crackled and the smoke curled toward the sky, something deeper stirred in me. I stood there in silence, watching years of tangled roots, thorns, and dry brush turn to ash. It wasn't just the physical weeds we had pulled—it felt like a funeral for some of the pain I had carried. Unspoken grief. Silent disappointments. Parts of my story I had tried to bury, but remained a weight within my spirit.

There was something strangely holy about standing by that fire. The air was thick with smoke, but it also felt sacred—like the Spirit of God was moving in that moment, unseen but undeniably present. I didn't have the words to name everything I was releasing, but my soul knew. This was more than a burn pile. This was surrender. We weren't just burning brush—we were laying down burdens. We were naming the things we couldn't carry anymore and trusting them to the flame. With each flicker of flame, it felt like God was whispering, "Let it go. I can handle this." And for the first time in a long time, I believed Him.

Later that evening, I found myself reflecting on what had happened, and I began to think about how often ashes show up in Scripture. Not just as what's left behind, but as a language of grief, of repentance, of surrender.

In times of deep sorrow, people would sit in ashes, sprinkle them on their heads, or wear sackcloth and ashes as a way of saying, "This hurts. I am undone." Job sat among the ashes in the depths of his suffering (Job 2:8). Mordecai, mourning the decree against his people, tore his clothes and covered himself in sackcloth and ashes (Esther 4:1). The prophet Jeremiah urged God's people to roll in ashes and wail with grief (Jeremiah 6:26). These moments mark more than just pain—they are sacred spaces where sorrow meets surrender, where hearts are laid bare before God.

But ashes weren't only for mourning. They also represented repentance—a posture of humility that said, "I have nothing to offer but my need for mercy." Daniel fasted and prayed in sackcloth and ashes (Daniel 9:3). The king of Nineveh responded to Jonah's warning by sitting in ashes, turning his heart back to God (Jonah 3:6). To sit in ashes was to say, "I'm not self-sufficient. I need grace."

Ashes also remind us of our mortality and dependence on God. Abraham humbly declared, "...I am nothing but dust and ashes..." (Genesis 18:27, NIV), and Ecclesiastes reminds us, "...all come from dust, and to dust all return" (Ecclesiastes 3:20, NIV). In the tradition of Ash Wednesday, we hear these same words—an invitation not to despair, but to remember that life is fragile, and God is faithful. From the dust He formed us. In the ashes, He meets us. And through His mercy, He brings beauty where we least expect it.

Scripture shows us a profound picture of ashes—not as our ending place, but as the place where God meets us. Isaiah 61:3 (NIV) paints a breathtaking picture of redemption: He gives "...a crown of beauty instead of ashes, the oil of joy instead of mourning, and a garment of praise instead of a spirit of despair." Ashes mark the place where grief meets surrender. But they are also holy ground, the very soil where healing begins.

The prophet Joel knew something about ashes, too.

The book of Joel begins with a vivid picture of devastation: the fields are ruined, the ground mourns, and the joy of the people has withered away. It's a scene of desolation—of things once full of life now reduced to dust. Joel calls the people to weep, to fast, to lament. It's not a quick fix or a bypass around pain. It's an honest, communal acknowledgment of loss.

But the story doesn't end there.

In Joel 2, God responds with a promise that echoes straight into our places of loss: "I will repay you for the years the locusts have eaten..." (Joel 2:25a, NIV). He doesn't offer shallow comfort or pretend the devastation didn't happen. He promises *restoration*. Beauty, joy, and new life *after* the ruin. It's the holy tension of grief and grace—God meets us in the ashes and begins the slow, sacred work of rebuilding.

And isn't that what surrender really is? It's not pretending everything's fine. It's bringing the ruins to God and trusting Him with the rebuild. It's believing that even if the years feel stolen, the harvest isn't over. There is still more to come.

In God's hands, what feels like the end becomes the starting point of something beautiful. I didn't fully grasp the weight of that promise until I saw it unfold in a way I could touch and hold. It was no longer just a verse on a page—it became part of my story.

*   *   *

Near the end of the week, Oswaldo came to find those of us who had been to the burn pile, offering to take us back to see what remained. The ashes had become a symbol of the work God was doing within us. When we arrived at the burn pile, Oswaldo had a small, clear, plastic zipper-top bag for each of us. After taking a few moments to be still before the Lord and acknowledging all that He had been doing in our hearts that week, we each filled our bags with ashes from the pile. These ashes became a tangible reminder of the truth Elisabeth Elliott eloquently writes, "Of one thing I am perfectly sure: God's story never ends with ashes."[11]

Though our pain was different, though the ashes represented something unique to each of us, we all felt overrun with pain, which was now reduced to embers. But even there, God was present. We began to see the ashes as a place to begin again. A place where hope began to bloom. And hope doesn't pretend the past didn't happen. It just believes the past isn't the whole story.

Shared Suffering, Shared Ashes

When I volunteered in the nursery at church, I served with a couple who had five children and had lost their home to fire. Everything they owned was gone in an instant. Returning to the site of a home that had once been a place of joy, laughter, and love was painful. Yet they remained faithful in believing God would provide for their every need. They grieved while also trusting God with the unknown. When we see something precious—a home, a marriage, a dream—reduced to ashes, we grieve not only what has been lost but also what will never be.

---

11 Elliot, *These Strange Ashes*, 12.

From the day my first husband put my wedding band on, I never took it off. Not for a shower, a massage, not even for surgery. To me, this ring symbolized a covenant made before God, and I held that promise close. Ironic, I suppose, when you consider the symbolic nature of the ring I had once worn bearing the words, "True Love Waits." Maybe subconsciously, I didn't want to remove my wedding ring because I had failed at "earning" and "being worthy" of the one symbolizing sexual purity. No matter the motivation, it had remained on my hand since the day he put it on in front of God, two pastors, and a church full of people. So seeing my marriage and dreams reduced to ashes, it felt like all was lost, including all that the wedding band stood for.

One day, as I sat in my pastor's office with my then-husband, twisting the wedding band on my finger, I felt a wave of peace come over me, and I knew this was the moment to finally take it off. I slowly slid the narrow gold band across my knuckle and placed it on the palm of my hand.

Looking down at this circle meant to symbolize infinite love and a commitment to one another, I turned to my husband and spoke with a trembling voice, "I have kept this ring on my finger since the day you placed it there as a symbol of the covenant we made before God and our pastors. Today, in the presence of God and our pastor, I acknowledge this ring represents vows that have been broken, and I choose to remove it as an acknowledgment that the covenant of marriage we once shared no longer exists. I don't know what the future holds, but I do know I do not want a marriage like ours had become."

A warm tear rolled down my cheek and landed on the palm of my hand holding what now felt like a meaningless piece of metal. I took in a deep breath and turned my eyes toward my pastor, who sat in an armchair across from me. He didn't flinch or rush to fill the silence. His eyes held a depth of sorrow that mirrored my own, as if he, too, felt the ache of what was being laid to rest. I think he saw traces of his own daughter in me, and that connection made the weight of my grief something he willingly stepped into, not just as a pastor, but almost as a father.

When he finally spoke, his voice was steady but thick with compassion. He affirmed my decision to remove my wedding ring and gently said, "You are a treasure worth fighting for." It wasn't just a statement—it was a shared lament, an acknowledgment of the sacred weight of grief. In that moment, he wasn't offering polished answers or distant encouragement. He was sitting *with* me in the ashes, bearing witness to the breaking and honoring the loss.

With those words, grief began to settle over my soul like a heavy blanket as I acknowledged my marriage was no more. But somehow, even in the sorrow, I didn't feel alone. His presence reminded me that this pain was seen, held, and shared—that God often shows up through others willing to sit beside us in the dark.

Grief often feels isolating, but the truth is—we all carry ashes. Some are visible, like the ruins of a burned-down home or a broken relationship. Others are tucked quietly behind smiles and busy schedules—unmet expectations, silent disappointments, or prayers still waiting for answers. Whether it's a friend navigating loss, a family member walking through illness, or our own private heartaches, suffering touches us all in different ways.

And yet, that shared space feels sacred—where individual sorrows become collective compassion. When we acknowledge our ashes, we not only give ourselves permission to grieve, but we extend grace to one another. The couple who lost their home, the young couple who lost a baby, the countless others carrying invisible weight—we are not alone in our mourning. In community, in honesty, and in faith, we discover that while our ashes may look different, the hope of restoration is the same. Because we worship a God who meets us in the ashes—not just to sit with us in sorrow, but to begin the healing work only He can do.

The Mosaic of the Broken

There's something about brokenness that begs for redemption. We want to believe that the pieces can be gathered, that the fire didn't consume everything, that beauty can still rise from the ruins. But healing isn't neat. It's not fast or polished. It's slow, worthy work. And as I sat with the ashes and all they represented, I began to realize that God wasn't asking me to forget the broken places—He was inviting me to see them differently. Not as evidence of failure or loss, but as material for something new.

That's when I started thinking about mosaics.

Nearly every vacation, my son finds an art museum (or three) for us to visit. We peruse every gallery and style of art imaginable, but perhaps one of my favorites is the gallery of mosaics. This beautiful art is made by assembling many small pieces into a larger, unified image or design. The process for creating mosaics is both intricate and intentional. They are made from broken pieces—tiny fragments and jagged shards. And yet, when they're placed with intention and care, they become something stunning. Meaningful. Whole. Mosaics serve as a reminder to us that brokenness doesn't cancel out beauty. Sometimes, it's the very thing beauty is built from.

Isn't that just like God? He's the Master Artist—the one who gathers our shattered dreams, our broken hearts, our painful memories—and doesn't toss them aside. He uses them. Every single piece. God starts with a vision—not of who we were in the mess, but of who we're becoming. He gathers every disappointment, every loss, every tear, and begins placing them with tenderness and purpose. Piece by piece, He's building something more beautiful than we can imagine.

You, my friend, are a mosaic in progress. Sometimes we think of ourselves as broken when really it's pieces of our story that are broken. Your brokenness isn't being tossed aside—it's being shaped, piece by piece, into a living testimony of a God who never wastes anything. He is the master of putting pieces back together in a more beautiful way. So let Him keep working. Let Him keep placing. And trust that even the sharpest shards in your story can shine in the masterpiece He's making.

But before the mosaic takes shape—before the broken pieces find their place—there's the breaking itself. The scattering. The sharp edges of loss that still sting when you touch them. We sit among the ashes. That's where grief first meets us—in the aftermath, when the breaking is still fresh and the beauty feels far off. But even the ashes—soft, weightless, and easily overlooked—can become part of the masterpiece. God doesn't sweep them away. He redeems them.

Good Grief

Grief isn't linear. It is not a checklist or a timeline. The stages of grief—denial, anger, bargaining, depression, and acceptance—don't arrive in order or wait their turn. Some days you're numb. Other days, you're angry, aching for answers, or desperate to re-write what happened. Some days, the sadness sits heavily. And other times, there's a strange peace that doesn't quite make sense—maybe even a moment of hope. That's all part of it.

Grief has a way of echoing beyond the moment.

One day, you might feel steady. The next, a memory sweeps in and knocks the breath right out of you. It reminds me of when you drop a pebble into the water, causing ripples that stretch across the whole body of water. When you drop a stone of loss into the water, the ripples reach places you didn't expect—how you trust, how you show up, how you see the world. Just when it seems like the water's calm, another ripple touches the shore. But those ripples? They're not proof that you're broken beyond repair. They're reminders that your grief runs deep.

And wherever grief finds you—God is already there.

There's no part of your pain too big for God. No depth He won't enter. He isn't overwhelmed by your emotions. He's not asking you to be "fine." He's simply asking you to bring it—to bring *you*—just as you are.

You're safe in His hands. And He's not done writing your story.

Dancing on Holy Ground

It was customary for visiting mission teams to create a sign to add to the posts on the ranch's property—a tradition that marked each group's presence like a quiet testimony etched into the landscape. Being from Nashville, our group brought a guitar-shaped sign with the name of our church and the number of miles between us and the ranch. What I didn't realize was that the very spot where our sign would be placed—the patch of ground chosen seemingly at random—was the same place where I had once sat and wept before the Lord among the thorns and dust.

The morning before we left the ranch, our team gathered there. We took turns using a permanent marker to sign the back of the guitar shape. Next, we gathered in a circle around it and prayed for the work God would continue to do at the school and in the hearts of the children attending it. Afterward, the sign was nailed to a large wooden post to be cemented back into the ground.

As we stood there—dust on our shoes, hearts full from the week—one of the men suggested we write the reference for Joshua 5:15 in the wet cement. Unfamiliar with the verse, I asked him to share what it said. He replied, "Take off your sandals, for the place where you are standing is holy" (NIV).

We knew we were standing on holy ground.

There was no delay. We paused again to pray together, and almost immediately, worship began to rise. The same man who shared the verse pulled out his guitar and began to lead us in song. One by one, we removed our shoes in reverence. The ground where we had once wept was now sacred. Our worship over the turned soil became a declaration—not just of faith, but of freedom. We stood, arms raised, praising God in the very place where pain was surrendered.

In these moments of worship, my mind turned to 1 Peter 1:6–7 (NIV):

> *In all this you greatly rejoice, though now for a little while you may have had to suffer grief in all kinds of trials. These have come so that the proven genuineness of your faith—of greater worth than gold, which perishes even though refined by fire—may result in praise, glory and honor when Jesus Christ is revealed.*

As we sang, something in me shifted. The weight I had been carrying all week lifted, and the worship pouring out of me felt different—lighter, truer. Spontaneously, one of the other women asked if I would join her in dancing as we continued to lift praise to God. No choreography. No restraint. Just barefoot joy in the dust. We danced in circles, kicked up the dry earth beneath us, and laughed through our tears. It felt like freedom. Like release. Like the most honest response to a God who had met us so intimately in our pain.

Just before heading back to finish up our work on the ranch, I paused and lifted my arms once more, whispering a prayer.

> *Thank You, God, for the work You have done in me on this holy ground. Thank You for reminding me I am not alone. Help me hold fast to the promise that You make all things new and work all things together for good. As I return home, keep my heart open to the work You are still doing in me. May something beautiful begin to bloom. In Jesus' name, Amen.*

As I stood with outstretched arms, one of the women snapped a photo of the shadow my arms cast over the weeds. It's one of my favorite pictures. You can't see me—only the silhouette of arms lifted in worship, despite the weeds… and perhaps, because of them.

What began as a place of mourning had become a place of rejoicing.

The Sacred Work of Surrender

With my small bag of ashes in tow and heart surrendered to God, I sat in the back of the van as it rumbled over the desert terrain and headed to the airport. Images from the week flashed in my mind, a montage of moments I would never forget. With each image came pulses of emotion within me—pain, grief, surrender, relief, freedom, peace, rejoicing. Driving away from the ranch felt like a release from it all. Like a surrender of the pain. But in the surrender, I did not feel discouraged or disheartened. Instead, for the first time in months, a pulse of hope now surged through me. In many ways, it felt like God had not only been turning the soil of brokenness in my heart, but He had walked me through the fire that week. What had felt like destruction now felt like a seedbed of hope.

I thought of Joel's words again: "You will have plenty to eat, until you are full, and you will praise the name of the Lord your God…" (Joel 2:26, NIV). What was once stripped bare had begun to bloom. And though I didn't yet know what the harvest would look like, I believed in the One who had planted hope in the ashes. I came to realize God's refining fire does not destroy—it reveals what's indestructible. And surrender does not mean defeat—it means placing the ashes into God's hands, believing He will bring restoration.

In her book, *Courage for the Unknown Season*, Jan Silvious writes, "Acknowledging the reality of your situation is critical, but that reality doesn't have to stop you from going forward."[12] For the first time since I learned of my then-husband's affair, I was able to acknowledge the reality—my marriage covenant no longer existed, and it was time to step forward in faith, trusting that God's story never ends with ashes.

In the days and weeks that followed our return from the ranch, I kept thinking about the ashes I had carried home. I had tucked that little bag into my suitcase, but it wasn't just soot—it was symbolic. It held the ache of what had been lost, the weight of what I had surrendered, and a whisper of hope for what might still be possible. I didn't know yet what God would do with all of it, but I knew He wasn't finished.

---

12 Silvious, Jan. *Courage for the Unknown Season: Navigating What's Next with Confidence and Hope.* Tyndale Momentum, 2017.

Beauty in BLOOM

Even when everything feels wasted, broken, or beyond repair, God's promise still stands.

He doesn't just see the ashes—He treasures what you've lost.

He promises not just survival but restoration.

Not just an ending, but a new beginning.

Not just memories of what was, but miracles of what will be.

Whisper this promise to your heart today:

Nothing is wasted in God's hands. He is already working to redeem what feels ruined.

B–Believe It

- Grief is holy. It's part of the refining, not something to avoid, but something to walk through with God.
- God never ends a story with ashes. He always brings beauty in time.
- Your brokenness is not wasted. It is where redemption begins.

L–Linger

- "In all this you greatly rejoice, though now for a little while you may have had to suffer grief in all kinds of trials. These have come so that the proven genuineness of your faith—of greater worth than gold, which perishes even though refined by fire—may result in praise, glory and honor when Jesus Christ is revealed" (1 Peter 1:6–7, NIV).

O–Observe

- Take a moment to reflect on a time in your life when something you had hoped for or dreamed of was reduced to ashes. Maybe it was a relationship, a job, a season of life, or even an expectation you had for yourself.

- How did that loss impact you emotionally, spiritually, or physically?
- Where did you see God in that season?
- Looking back now, can you see any ways that God was refining or reshaping you through that experience?
- What do you need to surrender today—something you're still holding onto, afraid to release to God?

O–Offer Prayer

Lord,

I come to You with hands open and heart heavy.

There are things I have lost—

dreams that have burned down,

relationships that have unraveled,

seasons I never wanted to end.

I bring You my ashes, Lord.

The pain.

The grief.

The pieces of a life I thought would look different.

You see every tear. You know every ache.

I lay it all at Your feet.

Even when I don't understand, I choose to trust.

Even when my heart trembles, I choose to believe You are still good.

Even here, in the smoke and ruin, I believe You are making something new.

You are the God who turns mourning into dancing,

ashes into beauty,

brokenness into purpose.

Refine me in the fire, Lord—not to destroy me,
but to make me whole in You.
Shape my story for Your glory.
Help me surrender what was, so I can receive what is to come.
And as I wait for the bloom after the burn,
help me rest in Your presence,
lean on Your promises,
and worship even here.
This is holy ground. I trust You with my ashes.
In Jesus' name, Amen.

M–Magnify

When you stand on the ground of your grief and worship anyway, you declare what Joel's people came to know: the wastelands will not have the final word. God will.

- If you feel led, stand up and physically move—walk, sway, or even dance—thanking God for His refining work, even in the midst of pain. (If possible, do this barefoot as a reminder, "...the place where you are standing is holy" (Joshua 5:15, NIV).

- Say a prayer of gratitude, thanking God for how far you have come. Praise Him for being ever-present and for the promise that He will bring beauty from your brokenness as He works all things for good.

5

Breath in the Valley

Learning to Breathe Through Grief and Change

"Reading the Bible is inhaling. Praying is exhaling."
— Dane C. Ortlund[13]

When Breath is Hard to Find

Breath is more than oxygen—it's evidence of life. And when life feels heavy, even the simple act of breathing becomes sacred. It becomes survival. A whispered prayer. A steadying rhythm when everything else feels out of sync.

There are times when we hold our breath out of fear, anticipation, or grief, and there are times when it's hard to catch our breath at all. I've experienced both.

I would say I am an average swimmer. Not particularly strong, but I am capable of moving about in the water unafraid. Well,

---

13 Ortlund, Dane C. *Deeper: Real Change for Real Sinners*. Crossway, 2021.

except that one time I saw a barracuda. I have never swum away so fast and afraid in all my life. You'd have thought I was trying to beat Olympian Michael Phelps in a race.

The only other time I remember being truly uncomfortable in the water was a day when I was about ten years old. I dove into the pool at the local country club, swam around near the bottom, then attempted to come up for air.

With my eyes closed, I pressed toward the surface of the water only to ram into a large, circular float with several people on it. I was trapped there and could not see the edge. Panic quickly set in as I frantically ran my hand along the underside of the float, attempting to find the edge and push the float up so those above would realize there was someone trapped underneath. Having expended much of my breath while swimming around, a brief thought crossed my mind: *I am about to drown. Lord, help me.*

Just as the prayer exhaled from within me, someone on the float must have realized I was trapped beneath it. There was a swift paddling from one side of the float, and finally, I could see the light of the sunshine glimmering on the water above. With what little energy I had left, I lifted my head to the surface and gasped for air. My breathing was rapid. Inhale. Exhale. Inhale. Exhale. It's a wonder I didn't hyperventilate and pass out. The breath filling my lungs had never felt so needed, so fresh, so life-giving.

I didn't realize how precious breath could feel until I almost lost it. That panic—of not knowing how much longer I could hold on—has come back to me in other moments, though not in a pool.

Grief has its own way of pressing down like a weight on the chest. Shame can feel like trying to come up for air, only to hit an invisible ceiling. Trauma doesn't announce itself politely; it slams into us, uninvited, and suddenly we're gasping. Struggling. Spiritually breathless.

There have been seasons where I've felt like I was swimming through sorrow, eyes closed, just trying to find the surface. But no matter how hard I reached or how fast I paddled, the clarity, the breath, felt just out of reach. Just as my lungs once burned for air, my soul has burned for hope. For healing. For something—*anything*—to make the ache stop.

It's in those moments I've learned: spiritual breath is just as necessary as physical breath. And just like that summer day in the pool, when I couldn't save myself, it wasn't my strength that got me through. It was God's mercy. A hand I couldn't see was making a way for me to rise again.

The psalmist captures this kind of rescue in vivid, breath-stealing imagery:

> *He reached down from on high and took hold of me;*
> *He drew me out of deep waters.*
>
> *(Psalm 18:16, NIV)*

That's what grace does. It finds us when we're flailing. It lifts us when we're spent. And it fills our lungs with hope when all we've known is gasping.

I am not afraid of the water as a result of being trapped under the float that day, but I tend to stay closer to the surface than I once did. Whether in a pool, lake, or ocean, I want to know that I can easily access a fresh breath of air at any given moment.

Breath is necessary for life, and how we breathe often mirrors the condition of our heart and mind. When we're anxious, our breath shortens. When we rest, it deepens. Likewise, when hope feels distant, our "spiritual breathing" can feel shallow, like we're just gasping through the day. But when we reconnect with God, our breath steadies. Our soul inhales truth and exhales trust.

Breath reminds us of the rhythm of faith: inhale His promises, exhale our burdens. Inhale His peace, exhale our striving. It's not a one-time thing. It's a moment-by-moment practice. And with each breath, we're reminded that God is as near as the air around us.

The Inhale: Reading the Bible

In my lowest moments, I found comfort in the book of Psalms. One verse in particular spoke to me the week of the mission trip:

> *Be gracious to me, God, be gracious to me,*
> *For my soul takes refuge in You;*
> *And in the shadow of Your wings I will take refuge*
> *Until destruction passes by.*
>
> *(Psalm 57:1, NASB)*

This verse holds a promise. Not only will God be a safe place of refuge, but we also find hope in the statement *"until destruction passes by."* There's an implied affirmation—the storm, the destruction, *will* come to an end. It *will* pass by. It will *not* last forever. This verse became my soul's inhale in times of distress. I clung to God, asking Him to be gracious to me, and when words failed me, scripture became my very way of breathing again.

Dane C. Ortlund describes spiritual breathing in this way: "Reading the Bible is inhaling. Praying is exhaling."[14] He goes on to explain:

> *Taking a big breath into our lungs fills us with fresh air, gives us oxygen, calms us down, provides focus, and brings mental clarity. What inhaling does for us*

---

14 Ortlund, *Deeper*, 76.

*physically, Bible reading does for us spiritually. In this shifty, uncertain world, God has given us actual words. Concrete, unmoving, fixed words. We can go to the rock of Scripture amid the shifting sands of this life. Your Bible is going to have the same words tomorrow that it does today. Friends can't provide that—they will move in and out of your life, loyal today but absent tomorrow. Parents and their counsel will die. Your pastor will not always be available to take your call. The counselor who has given you such sage instruction will one day retire, or maybe you'll move out of state. But you can roll out of bed tomorrow morning and, whatever stressors slide uncomfortably across your mental horizon as you groan with the anxieties of the day, your friend the Bible is unfailingly steady. It lies there, awaiting opening, eager to steady you amid all the unanswered questions before you that day. It will give you what you need and not evade you. Our truest wisdom and only safety is to build our lives on its words. (Matt. 7:24–27)*15

When all that was constant in my life had been removed, I found the reality of this observation to be true. God's Word, no matter what changed around me, remained constant, steady, and a source of life. Some mornings I would open my Bible to Psalm 34, reading the same lines again and again: "I sought the Lord, and He answered me; He delivered me from all my fears" (Psalm 34:4, NIV). That verse became breath in my lungs. And just as scripture became my inhale, prayer and praise became my exhale.

---

15 Ortlund, *Deeper*, 146.

The Exhale: Prayer and Praise

My alarm went off well before the sun. Our team had decided to climb what had been dubbed by the residents of the ranch as "Snoopy Rock" to watch the sunrise. Snoopy Rock was a large hill rising above the valley where the ranch was positioned. There was no clear path up its rocky face, but from the top, we were told, you could see the expanse of the ranch and beyond.

As we made our way up the jagged hill, step by step, dust and rocks shifting beneath our feet, there was a stillness, a silence, that swelled around us. It was still dark out, so the anticipation of the sunrise built throughout our climb.

Upon reaching the summit, we spread out, and each of us found a place to sit. Staring out over the valley, a small ray of light began to break through across the horizon. As the light continued to expand, beautiful colors of red and orange began to appear, and the rays grew in number, reaching like outstretched arms over the valley below.

As the ranch came into clearer view, it revealed a picture of God's faithfulness. A fresh perspective. Before, I could see only the weeds, thorns, and dust right before me as I sat in the valley— physically and spiritually. Now, however, it was as though I could see the ranch and the broad desert as God did. From above, the valley came into full view, and it was stunning. Seeing things from this new perspective, I was no longer focused on the imperfections, but on the beauty of the whole.

As exhausted as we all were from the physical labor of the week and the early alarms that morning, we still felt compelled to stand on the hilltop and worship the Lord. Worship, even in weakness, becomes our exhale. The psalmist writes, "Let everything that has breath praise the Lord" (Psalm 150:6, NIV). And that we did. We praised God *in* the valley; now we would also praise Him after it.

Facing the valley below, I lifted both hands to the sky. As I stood there, I whispered a prayer: *Lord, renew a right spirit within me. Pour out Your Spirit upon me and grant me Your peace that passes understanding. Keep my eyes open to how You're weaving even the valleys into the beauty of mountaintop moments.*

Prayer and praise became my exhale. And the more I turned to God, leaning into His Word and resting in His truth, the more I felt His breath filling my spirit.

The Breath of God

Growing up, my family was part of a drama troupe that traveled to churches and performed plays. My roles were often insignificant—one time, I even played a donkey in a Christmas production. Thank goodness social media did not yet exist. Though my roles were small, my parents wanted to include me in this meaningful ministry.

My dad was a co-director of the group. Each night before we took the stage, he would have us gather in a circle to pray before leading us in singing the hymn, "Spirit of the Living God." I can still hear our voices joined together singing these powerful words: "*Spirit of the Living God, fall afresh on me... melt me, mold me, fill me, use me.*"[16] At the time, I was too young to grasp their meaning. But as I began to walk through my healing journey, the lyrics took on a whole new life. These words became my prayer. My whole life, I had made plans. But that's just it. They were *my* plans, not God's.

---

16 Hawn, C. Michael. "History of Hymns: 'Spirit of the Living God.'" *Discipleship Ministries*, The United Methodist Church, 2013, https://www.umcdiscipleship.org/articles/history-of-hymns-spirit-of-the-living-god.

Now, with everything seemingly reduced to ashes, I turned my heart and my prayer to God, asking Him to melt me, mold me, fill me, and use me. This prayer was an act of surrender. Sometimes in my grief, I felt almost lifeless. But as I shifted my focus, asking the Living God to fall afresh on me, I felt the Holy Spirit breathe new life into my soul. I began to recognize God was not just protecting, but also shaping me, refining me, forming something new from the ashes.

Scripture is saturated with breath—divine, restorative, holy breath. God formed Adam from the dust of the earth—ordinary, lifeless particles—until the breath of the Almighty filled his lungs and brought life to his body (Genesis 2:7). That same breath—the Spirit of God—still breathes into us today. In Job 33:4 (NIV), we read, "The Spirit of God has made me, and the breath of the Almighty gives me life." In Ezekiel, the prophet sees a vision of dry bones in a valley—lifeless, scattered remains. But God says, "I will make breath enter you, and you will come to life" (Ezekiel 37:5, NIV). And so He does. Breath becomes prophecy. Restoration. Resurrection.

Jesus, too, breathes life into His disciples: "And with that He breathed on them and said, 'Receive the Holy Spirit'" (John 20:22, NIV). It's not dramatic. It's intimate. Quiet. Breath has always been God's delivery system for presence. For power.

The same breath that filled Adam's lungs, that revived a valley of bones, that fell fresh upon the disciples, is still at work in us. When we feel worn thin by grief, disappointment, or disillusionment, God's breath becomes our revival. His Spirit sustains us when our own strength fails. His breath is not just life-giving; it's hope-restoring. It is transformational.

The Paradox: The Valley of Vision

In the first year following my divorce, a friend from my church led me through the Bible study *Gospel Transformation*.[17] I've shared before how powerful community is in healing, and this friend took that calling seriously. Each week, she came to my apartment and walked with me through the next lesson—sometimes through tears, sometimes through silence, but always with grace. Bit by bit, I began to see all that had transpired in my marriage, divorce, and the days that followed not merely as destruction but as the beginning of transformation.

I had written before about breath in the valley, and now, I was living it. Each week with my friend was a steadying rhythm of grace. It was like inhaling truth and exhaling sorrow. No rush. No pressure. Just the slow return of life where grief had once taken up all the space. That's how the Lord moves—quietly, redemptively, often through what feels like reversal.

This is the way of the Lord. The paradox of the Kingdom of God. Down is the way up.

Scripture is full of these divine reversals:

- *Surrender leads to freedom* (Matthew 11:28–30; Luke 9:23–24)

- *Suffering produces joy* (James 1:2)

- *The first shall be last, and the last shall be first* (Matthew 20:16)

- *Strength is found in weakness* (2 Corinthians 12:9)

- *Greatness is found in humility and service* (Mark 10:43)

---

17 Williams, Neil H. *Gospel Transformation: A 36-Lesson Inductive Study on the Transforming Power of the Gospel.* World Harvest Mission, 2006.

- And the very Son of God entered the world not as a king on a throne, but as a baby in a manger (Isaiah 9:6; Luke 2:1–7)

The truth that God gives beauty for ashes is also a holy paradox (Isaiah 61:3, NIV). Brokenness and beauty can—and often do—coexist.

One of the prayers that gave language to this mystery for me comes from a collection of Puritan prayers titled *The Valley of Vision*.

> *Lord, you have brought me to the valley of vision*
> *Where I live in the depths but see you in the heights;*
> *Hemmed in by mountains of sin I behold your glory*
> *Let me learn by paradox that the way down is the way up*
> *That to be low is to be high*
> *That the broken heart is the healed heart*
> *That the contrite spirit is the rejoicing spirit,*
> *That the repenting soul is the victorious soul,*
> *That to have nothing is to possess all,*
> *That to bear the cross is to wear the crown,*
> *That to give is to receive,*
> *That the valley is the palace of vision.*[18]

That prayer echoed what I was living. The valley—painful as it was—became sacred ground. It wasn't where I expected to find vision, let alone healing. But there, in the quiet ache of surrender, I began to see God differently. I began to see *myself* differently.

---

18 *The Valley of Vision: A Collection of Puritan Prayers and Devotions.* Edited by Arthur Bennett, The Banner of Truth Trust, 1975.

As Bob Goff writes in *Love Does*, "I used to think I could shape the circumstances around me, but now I know Jesus uses circumstances to shape me."[19]

That was it. I couldn't fix what had broken. I couldn't rewind the clock or rewrite the story. But Jesus could redeem it. He was shaping something new in me—not in spite of the pain, but through it.

This is the mystery of God's Kingdom: how surrender leads to freedom, how grief can give way to joy, how a valley that feels like a place of endings can become the beginning of something sacred.

The valley may feel forgotten, but it isn't forsaken. God is still present. He is still breathing. He is still creating beauty from the dust. Even when we can't see it, His breath sustains us. His Spirit whispers life into places we thought were done growing. The valley, it turns out, is where resurrection often begins, and we are finally able to take a full breath again.

---

19 Goff, Bob. *Love Does: Discover a Secretly Incredible Life in an Ordinary World.* Thomas Nelson, 2012.

Beauty in BLOOM

B–Believe It

- Destruction will pass by. This is not forever. The storm has a season.
- Worship brings clarity. Praise helps us see the valley as a place God never left.

L–Linger

- "Be gracious to me, O God, be gracious to me, for my soul takes refuge in You; and in the shadow of Your wings I will take refuge until destruction passes by" (Psalm 57:1, NASB).

O–Observe

- What does "refuge" look like for you right now?
- Can you recall a moment when God's presence felt like breath—subtle, sustaining, but sure?
- What parts of your life feel like they are "in the valley"? What beauty can you begin to notice even there?

O–Offer Prayer

- Breathe in Scripture: Close your eyes, take a deep breath, and slowly exhale. Repeat this process a few times. Then, as you breathe, meditate on Psalm 57:1.
  Inhale: *"Be gracious to me, O God, be gracious to me..."*
  Exhale: *"...for my soul takes refuge in You."*

M–Magnify

- Create a Breath Prayer Card: Write out Psalm 57:1 or another verse that speaks to you in this season. On the back of the card, write a simple breath prayer—just a few words you can pray as you inhale and exhale. For example:
  Inhale: "You are my refuge."
  Exhale: "I rest in You."

- Keep this card in your journal, wallet, or by your bedside. Return to it when breath feels hard to find—let it anchor you in God's presence, even in the valley.
- As you practice this, ask God to fill your breath with peace, your thoughts with truth, and your spirit with the awareness that He is near.

6

Tilling the Ground Through Therapy
Co-Laboring with God in the Deep Work of Healing

"You can walk hand in hand with both Jesus and a therapist. In fact, you are doing the bravest thing of all by allowing someone in who can walk you through the hard things. We were never meant to go on this journey alone."
— Tabitha Yates[20]

Preparing the Soil

There is a moment when the earth must break before anything can grow. It doesn't look like progress. It looks like loss, like disruption. But any gardener will tell you that growth doesn't begin with blooming; it begins with broken ground. The soil must be turned over and made soft. Left untouched, it stays too hard for roots to take hold.

---

20 Yates, Tabitha. *Jesus and Therapy.* Amazon Kindle ed., Independently published, 2023.

The same is true for the soul.

Before healing takes place, before transformation unfolds, something in us must break open. Sometimes it's our pride. Sometimes it's our illusion of control. Sometimes it's simply our silence finally giving way to honesty.

As we read in Hosea, "Sow righteousness for yourselves, reap the fruit of unfailing love, and break up your unplowed ground; for it is time to seek the Lord..."
(Hosea 10:12, NIV).

Break up your unplowed ground. It's not just a call to change. It's a call to begin again. To let God till the hardened places of our hearts. Not to shame us, but to restore us. The ashes that settle over our lives don't have to be the end of the story. With God, they can become fertilizer for something new. Something holy.

Breaking ground isn't easy. It's not tidy or predictable. It's disruptive. It's painful in ways we don't always have words for. It can feel like losing your footing, like standing in a place that's unfamiliar and vulnerable. All you may know is that the old ground no longer holds.

But it's also necessary, marking the beginning of restoration. It's God's invitation to trust, to soften, to surrender the hard and unyielding places of our hearts and let Him do His holy work.

Sometimes we think growth begins with strength. But so often, it begins with surrender. It's tempting to resist the breaking. To harden against it. But hardness only delays healing and growth. The ground of our hearts was never meant to stay unturned. The plow doesn't move gently; it breaks through what's become compacted over time. And yet God is not careless with the soil of our hearts.

He is intentional. Compassionate. He breaks what needs to be broken so that something new can be planted. Something lasting.

Therapy became the breaking ground. It was the place where the packed-down soil of my past began to shift. Where buried grief and tangled beliefs were slowly unearthed by truth spoken out loud. It wasn't easy. It wasn't pretty. But it was holy. And it was healing.

It takes courage to let someone step into the tender places of your story—to walk with you through the mess instead of pretending it doesn't exist. But that's what therapy did. It helped till the soil of my heart, clearing space for God to do what only He can do: plant something new, and grow something beautiful.

Facing What's Been Buried

Oddly enough, I didn't first walk into therapy because I felt broken. I walked in because my then-husband told me I needed help and was a "jealous wife" when I dared to ask if he was hiding an affair. My suspicions had risen to the surface, and this was probably a year before the truth came out. So, believing that maybe my insecurity really had just gotten the best of me, I took his advice and started going regularly to speak to someone I hoped could help "fix" me.

I felt like I shouldn't need this kind of help as a Christ follower. *Shouldn't my faith be enough? Shouldn't I be able to pray and have God heal me? Is this mental torment something I deserve because of my past?* It added another layer of shame before I ever set foot in the therapist's office.

And sadly, that shame wasn't just personal. It was also cultural—spiritual. The truth is, many of us grew up in church environments that never talked about counseling in a positive light. If therapy was mentioned at all, it was often with a side of suspicion, as if admitting you needed outside help meant you didn't trust God enough. Some even implied that Christians who struggled with mental health just needed more prayer, more faith, more obedience.

But what if healing isn't a betrayal of faith? What if it's a brave expression of it? What if sitting with a counselor is one of the ways we actually *live out* the belief that God cares about our whole selves—mind, body, and spirit?

We would never shame someone for going to the doctor to treat a broken bone. Why then do we shame ourselves or others for seeking help to heal a broken heart or a wounded soul?

That cultural silence around counseling made it all the harder to reach out, but also all the more necessary. Healing takes courage. And sometimes, it starts with sitting in the discomfort of asking for help, even when your heart is tangled in doubt and shame. Despite the deflection and blame hidden beneath his words, when my former husband said I needed help, he had pushed me toward the very healing God intended.

I sat in a tiny brick building, face-to-face with a stranger, baring my soul and wondering how I had gotten here: *What is wrong with me? Why can't I get past the past? Why do I still feel like I am not enough? Am I projecting my own pain onto my husband?* For the first time outside of the context of prayer, I sat and confessed *all* the things. The hurt, the shame, the sin, the guilt, the jealousy, the insecurity, the fear...every single bit.

Before long, the therapist recommended that my husband join me on the couch. With fear about what may come to light, I wrestled up the courage to invite him to one of my sessions. As we sat and talked *yet again* about the fact that I had not been a virgin when we got married, the therapist said, "I think you two are beating a dead horse." In that moment, I felt seen and heard for the first time. To hear someone else see this as something to release and move past lifted a weight from my shoulders, or started to anyway.

As she continued digging deeper with us on the topic, I'll never forget the moment she said, "Yours is a marriage in crisis. I believe a period of separation is necessary for you to move forward toward healing." This truth-telling, shining a light in the darkness, was met with incredible resistance.

Livid at the suggestion of separation, my then-husband jumped up from the couch, then raised his voice and said, "You're supposed to be a Christian counselor! How could you suggest separation? We all know separation leads to divorce, and divorce is not an option!" With that, he stormed from the room, slamming the door behind him. I sat dumbfounded by his response. *How could he respond that way? Was he not truly open to help? Was our marriage doomed if we couldn't come together to get the much-needed help of therapy?*

My therapist could see the rush of fear, shock, and gut-deep pain I felt as I processed what had just transpired. She spoke words of affirmation I had long needed to hear, "This is not your fault. He is upset because there is more to this story. There is more than what he is willing to share. Please do not continue to carry the guilt and shame around having premarital sex. And please consider physical separation to allow yourself space to heal."

Therapy tills more than current pain. It loosens long-buried layers of religious and cultural shame. For me, this conversation was the first moment I believed the shame I held close was not something God intended for me to carry. If God was willing to move past what He'd already forgiven, why was I still clutching the guilt like a souvenir?

I left the therapist's office that day and never saw her again. I wish I had. I needed to spend more time unpacking the layers of pain and doing the valid, helpful work that therapy provides. But in my fear and insecurity, I did not return, afraid that if I did, my marriage would surely end. Equally afraid that my need for therapy was the result of a lack of faith in what God could do.

The Deep Work

I could not have been more wrong. Following the revelation of my then-husband's infidelity, the church where he was on staff accepted his resignation and graciously covered my weekly counseling costs for three months of crisis care. I am not sure I would have made it had it not been for those many hours spent talking with a therapist.

These weekly sessions, like tilling hard ground, were slow and painful, but something in me started to give way. I remember sitting on that couch thinking, *"What if I open all this up and nothing changes?"* Some days, I wanted to bolt, thinking, *"Maybe it's easier to stay numb than to feel everything I've buried."* But the truth was, I had already been carrying the weight for too long. Slowly, I began to let it surface. And as I did, a tenderness began replacing the numbness.

One of the most powerful moments in my healing journey happened in a therapist's office with nothing more than a pen, a piece of paper, and a whole lot of emotion. My therapist invited me to write a letter to my then-husband—not to send, but to say the things I had never been able to voice. I poured out the grief, the anger, the confusion, the betrayal—everything I held inside. Page after page, I let the truth spill out raw and unfiltered.

When I was finished, she looked at me and said, "Now, I want you to tear it up." I stared at the pages for a moment, hesitant. But as I began to rip the letter into pieces, something broke loose in me. It wasn't about erasing the past; it was about releasing it. With each tear, I was letting go of the pain I had carried far too long. I was symbolically surrendering the hurt to God, trusting that He could hold it better than I ever could. That simple act didn't solve everything, but it marked a shift. A step toward freedom. A moment of saying, "This pain is real, but it doesn't get to define me anymore." It was a turning point, where healing began to take root in a new way.

The posture of my heart shifted as I realized therapy is not something else to be ashamed of. Seeking counsel isn't a sign of weak faith; it's a reflection of biblical wisdom and strength. The counsel of others is a resource God has provided for our healing. In her book *Jesus and Therapy: Bridging the Gap Between Faith and Mental Health*, Tabitha Yates speaks to this:

> *You can walk hand in hand with both Jesus and a therapist. In fact, you are doing the bravest thing of all by allowing someone in who can walk you through the hard things. We were never meant to go on this journey alone…In His Word, God demonstrates that receiving advice, guidance, and counsel is admirable, recommended, and beneficial. God is always working, and often He uses people to accomplish His purposes on earth.*[21]

Scripture reminds us, time and again, that wisdom, healing, and strength are rarely found in isolation. While prayer is powerful and essential, we're also called to seek out partnership—through mentors, counselors, pastors, therapists, and trusted friends. These relationships aren't just helpful. They're deeply biblical.

---

21 Yates, Tabitha. *Jesus and Therapy.* Amazon Kindle ed., Independently published, 2023.

Proverbs paints this picture clearly: "For lack of guidance a nation falls, but victory is won through many advisers" (Proverbs 11:14, NIV). It's a striking image. Victory hinging not on solitary effort, but on the counsel of many. God often leads us toward healing through the wisdom and care of others.

Therapy can be a place where godly counsel helps us process pain, explore truth, and move forward with clarity. Sometimes, we can't reach the depths of our own hearts without help. Proverbs speaks to this as well: "The purposes of a person's heart are deep waters, but one who has insight draws them out" (Proverbs 20:5, NIV). A wise therapist or counselor rooted in compassion and discernment can help draw out what we've buried or struggled to name.

We were never meant to journey alone. Galatians 6:2 calls us to a shared life: "Carry each other's burdens, and in this way you will fulfill the law of Christ" (NIV). Therapy is one way we invite another to help carry the weight with us—not because we are weak, but because we were created for connection. Together, we become more whole. Not by striving alone, but by opening our hearts to others, especially those equipped to help us see, grow, and heal.

Even as therapy helped me unearth old lies and lean into grace, healing didn't come in easily. There were days I felt like I was moving forward, and days I felt buried beneath the weight of survival. Healing is holy, yes. But sometimes, it is also heavy.

The Weary Soul: When Healing Feels Heavy

I have struggled with anxiety for years. I can't really pinpoint when it began, but it escalated in the years following my divorce, eventually leading to panic attacks.

I'll never forget my first one. Everything felt like it was coming to a head. Finances. Single motherhood. The daily stress of teaching. The pressure to be everything for everyone. It was around eleven o'clock that evening when I received a text message from a parent of one of my students that sent me spiraling. I can't remember exactly what it said, but I remember it triggering the feeling, yet again, that I could never be enough. Under normal circumstances, a message like this wouldn't have been a big deal, but this time it was the straw that broke the camel's back. All the feelings of not being enough crashed in at once. I pleaded with God, "*What more can I do?*"

As tears began to fall, there was a sudden tightening in my chest, and I felt myself gasping for air. I literally thought I might be dying. I backed up against the wall of my bedroom and slid to the floor, clutching my chest and hyperventilating. I couldn't even eke out a single word. My son, around ten years old at the time, was asleep in bed. All I could picture was him finding me collapsed on the ground.

Fear had its grip on me. The weight of responsibility settled on me as if gravity had a stronger pull than before. It was more than that, though. My eyes were opened to all I had been carrying. The pain of rejection, shame, fear, and unfulfilled dreams weighed me down—emotionally, mentally, and now physically.

The next visit to my therapist's office, as I shared about the anxiety that had overcome me, we discussed the possibility of prescribing an antidepressant. By this point in my journey, God had been opening my eyes to see resources such as therapy and medication not as something to be ashamed of, but rather as something to receive as a step in my healing process, as something necessary. I came to see therapy and the medication that prevented my panic attacks as a gift. God was teaching me that healing isn't something we achieve. It's something we receive.

You've probably heard the story of the man stranded on his roof during a flood. A rowboat, a motorboat, and a helicopter came, and he refused them all, waiting on God. When he drowned and asked why God didn't save him, God said, "I sent you help three times."

The man had been blind to the gifts God had placed before him, when all along God was the very one providing the means of transportation to safety. Sometimes, we're so focused on expecting a dramatic, divine intervention that we miss the very real, practical ways God is moving on our behalf. He does hear our cries and help, but often through people, resources, and opportunities that we hadn't expected.

When my therapist talked to me about medication, I had a choice to make. I could be like the man on the roof, refusing what was before me, standing firm in my old belief that faith should be enough. Or, I could acknowledge that God was providing the means to heal what I could not. With that in mind and a prayer of thanksgiving, I started on medication.

Years later—yes, I am still taking medication—I had a conversation with my therapist. I had inadvertently forgotten to take my medication some days and had gotten into the habit of only taking it every couple of days. (This is *not* recommended. Always follow the direct instruction of the prescriber.) Feeling like I had things under control, I casually told her that I thought I could probably just wean off of it. She seemed surprised and questioned me, "Why would you want to do that when it's been working well to keep you in a healthy state?"

As I explained my unconventional way of taking the medicine in those recent days, her eyes widened. I went on to explain, "I don't want to become dependent on it. I want to be able to regulate myself in a healthy way."

She stopped me in my tracks. "First, you need to take the medicine as prescribed. Second, let me ask you…why are you concerned about being dependent on it? If I told you that you had a heart condition that required medication, would you tell me, 'No thanks, I don't want to be dependent on it? I'll just try to will myself to get better.'?" Ugh. She got me there. She has a way of doing that.

"Well, no." I meekly replied.

She went on to explain, "The medication you are taking is essentially for a misfire in your brain. You can't will it away. It's not something in your control, but the medicine can correct it." Faced with this truth, I knew she was right. If I stopped taking the medication, I would be like the man on the roof refusing the help offered to him and risk drowning in my own pride and anxiety.

Faith in God isn't about refusing help. It's about trusting that God can work *through* the help. Faith says, *"God is my Healer."* But it also says, *"God may heal through medicine, through therapy, through the wisdom of professionals He's equipped for this very purpose."* It's not an either/or. It's a both/and.

Scripture is full of examples where God uses ordinary means to bring about extraordinary outcomes:

- *He fed Elijah through a raven* (1 Kings 17).
- *He healed Naaman through muddy river water* (2 Kings 5).
- *Jesus healed the blind man using spit and mud* (John 9).

In each case, the healing came through something tangible, physical, even messy. That doesn't make it less divine; it makes it more relatable. It reminds us that God isn't limited to the miraculous. He often works through the mundane.

Therapy didn't erase my pain. It helped me name it, grieve it, and offer it to God. I didn't know it then, but that moment on the floor, gasping for breath as I had a panic attack, clinging to hope, was also a kind of breaking. Not a breakdown of faith, but a breakthrough in trust. God was gently tilling the soil, even through panic and fear, preparing me for something I couldn't yet see.

Healing is holy. And holy doesn't always look polished. Sometimes, it looks like letting go of everything we're trying so hard to hold together. I had always assumed God would meet me once I had it all together. But instead, He knelt beside me in the mess.

Signs of a New Season

I didn't walk out of therapy with all the answers. If anything, I walked out with more questions, but they were different now. Softer, less accusing. I wasn't demanding to know *why* everything had happened. I was beginning to ask *What now?* That was new.

Some days, I still felt scraped raw. There were sessions where I'd sit in my car afterward, staring at the steering wheel, too tired to drive. But other days I felt something stir. Not joy, not yet. But maybe the absence of numbness. A flicker of tenderness toward myself. A little more room to breathe.

There was one week, I remember, when I laughed at something and caught myself. It had been so long since laughter didn't feel like pretending. I sat with that moment longer than I needed to, surprised by how unfamiliar it felt to be light, even for a second.

Another time, I caught myself praying, not out of desperation, but out of hope. Just a few words. But they weren't bitter. I wasn't trying to force God to show up. I just wanted to talk with Him. That, too, felt like something new growing.

It wasn't dramatic. There was no great revelation. Just the slow realization that I didn't hate myself as much. That I didn't feel as helpless. That I could sit with pain without collapsing under it. It felt like the soil of my life had been turned over—still messy, still unsettled—but no longer dead. And in some way, it felt ready for whatever was to come next.

I thought of that line from Hosea, "...break up your unplowed ground..." (Hosea 10:12, NIV). For years, I'd resisted that breaking. I thought it meant loss. Now, I could see the mercy in it. I wasn't broken in the way I had thought. I was *brokenhearted*, and it had hardened my heart. But you can't plant in hard earth. And now something had shifted. Not blooming yet, but sprouting. The first green shoots.

The ground of my life was still tender, but it was no longer barren. I was beginning to believe that healing might come. Not all at once, but over time. And deep down, I sensed it: the same God who broke the ground hadn't left. He was staying. He was watering. He would be faithful to tend the new thing He was doing within me.

Maybe you, too, are in a place where your heart feels hardened. Don't be afraid of the breaking. Don't be afraid to dig deep and surrender. Because even in the breaking, even in the sowing, even in the waiting, God is faithful. Let the soil turn. Let the tears fall. Let the light in. God is not just near—He is tending to your soul with care. It may not look like growth yet, but this softening is the sign that something beautiful is on its way.

Beauty in BLOOM

B–Believe It

- Therapy is not a betrayal of faith. It's a brave expression of it.
- Healing isn't something we achieve. It's something we receive.
- God is not careless with the soil of your soul. He breaks what needs to be broken so something new can be planted.

L–Linger

- Reread Hosea 10:12 slowly.
- Let the image of "unplowed ground" settle. Ask yourself: What in me has grown hardened? Where is God inviting softness?

O–Observe

- What parts of your story have stayed buried because they felt too painful or too heavy to face?
- Have you ever believed that needing help meant your faith wasn't strong enough? Where might that belief have come from?
- What signs, however small, might show that healing is beginning, even if it's not yet blooming?
- Have you confused strength with self-sufficiency? What would it look like to see surrender as spiritual strength?
- In what ways might God be tilling the soil of your heart through therapy, community, or unexpected means?

O–Offer Prayer

God, I confess the places in me that feel hardened
by shame, fear, control, or pride.

I don't always understand the breaking,
but I trust that You are a gentle Gardener.
Till the soil of my soul, Lord.
Loosen what's buried.
Soften what's brittle.
I offer You my pain and ask for Your healing
through whatever means You choose to use.
Thank You for not leaving me in the wilderness
but for walking with me toward restoration.
I believe You are still watering. Still tending. Still near.
In Jesus' name, Amen.

M–Magnify

- Share what God is doing in your life, even if it's still in process.
- Post a reflection, journal a testimony, or simply whisper this truth aloud: *"Even the breaking can be beautiful when God is the One doing the planting."*
- You might also encourage others by sharing how God has used counseling, community, or unexpected resources to start healing work in you. Magnify the God who doesn't wait for us to bloom to call us beloved.

7

The Planting
Trading Sorrow for Hope

---

*"Trust that God is the God of your season, no matter
what it looks like, no matter how unknown."*
—Jan Silvious[22]

Trusting God in the Unknown

There's a kind of faith required when you plant a seed. You press something small and fragile into the earth with no guarantee of what will come of it. You can't see the roots forming or the growth happening underground. It's a bit messy, a bit mysterious, and often more like walking blindly into the unknown than confidently stepping into the light.

This realization hit me one day as I found myself deep inside a cave, surrounded by silence and darkness, unsure of each step and relying only on a voice ahead to guide me.

---

22 Silvious, Jan. *Courage for the Unknown Season: Navigating What's Next with Confidence and Hope.* Thomas Nelson, 2017.

We had been warned that we'd encounter tight spaces, uneven footing, and places where the mud would grab hold. I considered myself pretty adventurous, but descending further into the earth, I felt a quiet dread settle over me. The light from the entrance disappeared quickly. Everything felt foreign. It was dark, damp, and eerily quiet.

As we gradually made our way through the cave, there was a moment when my foot plunged knee-deep into the mud. It was thicker than I expected, and as I tried to move, I felt a resistance pull at my leg like a force trying to hold me there. It wasn't just the mud. I was sinking into my own fear, the kind that clings and whispers, *You're not going to make it out of this.* My heart pounded. Panic tugged at the edges of my calm. I glanced around, but the darkness offered no answers. *What if I get stuck? What if no one hears me? Is this really the path?*

I gripped the back of my thigh and pulled upward, trying to free my leg from the thick, clinging muck. It took effort. And courage. Because even when I couldn't see the way forward, I could still hear the guide calling out to keep going.

I remembered what he said before we began: "*Trust me to lead you. Listen for my voice. I will not leave you.*"

Trust. That word again. Something I've struggled with. Yet here, in the darkness and the unknown, I had no choice but to trust my guide. My instincts wanted certainty, a clear way forward. But all I had was his voice, and that had to be enough.

That experience reminded me how often God leads us through seasons much like that cave. We can't see beyond the next step. The path isn't always clear. Fear tries to take over. But God says the same thing to us that my guide did: "*Trust Me to lead you. Listen for My voice. I will not leave you.*"

That same invitation to trust would echo again—not in the darkness of a cave, but under the bright, unyielding lights of a courtroom. Different setting, same uncertainty. Once more, I could not see beyond the next step, and once more, I would have to steady my heart, listen carefully, and move forward.

* * *

"Are you sure you want to go through with this?"

That is what my former husband whispered to me as I sat beside him on a hard pew in the courtroom, waiting for our names to be called. His words were so unexpected that they sent a jolt through me as though I had been stunned with a taser. Could he be serious? We'd had countless conversations, pastoral counseling, and legal mediation leading up to this moment, so I didn't have to think very long about my response. I turned to him and, in an even tone with conviction in my spirit, said, "I am certain."

Moments later, the judge signed the divorce decree. Relief rose in me like a breath I hadn't realized I was holding, yet beneath it, sorrow quickly settled in. "I can't believe it's done. I don't know what to do now," I told my sister, my words heavy with both certainty and loss. I knew the choice to leave was right, and the freedom from an unhealthy marriage was real. But as we walked to her car outside the courthouse, a different weight pressed in: grief for what had been and uncertainty for what would come. A flood of thoughts ran through me: *What will my life look like as a single mom? How am I going to provide for my son on a teacher's income? Will my son push away, upset that he now has two homes? Is he going to be okay? Am I going to be okay? Will I ever marry again, or will I be alone the rest of my life?*

In the moment, I was seeing everything as loss. I felt so unsure of myself as I stared into an uncertain future. I'll never forget my brother-in-law speaking this truth to me, "You always want to plan seventeen steps ahead. But you don't have to do that. You just need to take this moment by moment. One step at a time." He was right. I was looking too far down the road, and that led to anxiety, fear, guilt, and uncertainty.

I carried silent shame, not just over the divorce itself, but over the fact that I couldn't fix what was broken. I felt like I'd failed at something God values deeply. But the truth is, God didn't ask me to be perfect—only present, willing to surrender. And when I did, He didn't meet me with condemnation. He met me with comfort. With presence. With peace.

Have you ever felt that kind of invisible shame? The kind that whispers, "You should have done more," or "You're the reason this failed"? If so, let me gently remind you: your value isn't measured by what you couldn't hold together. It's anchored in the One who still holds you now.

Ironically, in the same way I thought I had my whole life planned out—and God undid it all to bring His better plan to fruition—I found myself grasping for control yet again, wanting to have it all figured out. But that's not what faith is.

God didn't want me to know every step. He wanted me to trust Him to bring beauty from the ashes. I needed to stop striving and start surrendering. Once I did, I never could have imagined that what seemed like a loss would become an unexpected gift.

While it took some time to have a shift in my perspective, I have come to thank God for the very things I once begged Him to remove.

Looking back now, I see what I couldn't see then. What I was walking through wasn't just hardship; it was the testing of my faith. The refining. The deep work of God that doesn't always show up in the form of immediate answers, but in long, slow growth. James says it like this:

"Consider it pure joy, my brothers and sisters, whenever you face trials of many kinds, because you know that the testing of your faith produces perseverance. Let perseverance finish its work so that you may be mature and complete, not lacking anything"
(James 1:2–4, NIV).

At the time, I wouldn't have called it "joy." I might've called it survival. But now I can see:

That trial was producing something eternal.

That perseverance was building something I couldn't yet perceive.

God wasn't punishing me. He was preparing me.

And in His mercy, He didn't just get me through that season. He gave me a gift I never expected: a deeply connected relationship with my son.

We had so much one-on-one time, just the two of us, day after day, thanks to the parenting plan that kept him with me most of the time. I became intentional with my parenting. Present. Prayerful. The time we shared was meaningful and joyful, and I wouldn't trade it for anything.

In fact, I now say prayers of thanksgiving for those very years I once feared. God provided in every way—from extra income right down to the last cent of a bill. My son didn't push away; he drew closer. And the wounds I carried into single motherhood began to heal, not because everything was easy, but because God was faithful.

That's the beauty of healing. Healing looks like gratitude for what God has grown in the scorched places. Faith refined. Hope restored. Joy rediscovered.

Even though I didn't know what the future held, I began to release the need to have everything mapped out and instead started to trust God more with each passing day. Scripture tells us, "For we walk by faith, not by sight" (2 Corinthians 5:7, NASB). But let's be honest. Walking without sight isn't easy. It's vulnerable. It strips away control. And yet, it's often in the darkness that faith is formed.

Joshua is a powerful example of this kind of faith. Taking over after Moses wasn't just a leadership promotion. It was a call to walk through a wilderness of unknowns. He didn't get a detailed roadmap. He got a promise: "...the Lord your God will be with you wherever you go" (Joshua 1:9, NIV).

The weight of leadership. The grief of transition. The fear of the unknown. It was heavy, but it didn't disqualify him. It prepared him. God didn't need Joshua to see the entire plan. He needed him to follow with faith.

Much like the cave hid the path until the guide's voice drew me forward, the soil keeps its quiet work concealed until new life breaks through. Faith asks us to trust the unseen, to believe that in places where light feels scarce and movement feels messy, God is still guiding the growth. He is using the stuck seasons to forge a deeper dependence on Him. Not one built on answers, but one shaped when the path disappears and God remains.

Seeds, Soil, and Restoration

The days, weeks, and months following my divorce reminded me of my cave experiences. It felt like I was walking forward without a light or a clear path. Just a voice. Just a flicker of belief that maybe God was still leading. I felt unsure of myself and, if I'm honest, unsure at times whether I could even trust God.

One line from *Courage for the Unknown Season* by Jan Silvious stayed with me long after I closed the book: "Trust that God is the God of your season, no matter what it looks like, no matter how unknown."[23]

Being a divorced, single mom was never part of the map I'd made for my life. It wasn't a season I saw coming, and it certainly wasn't one I felt prepared for. My faith, once so sure, suddenly felt like shaky ground. I prayed constantly, but underneath those prayers was a lingering ache of uncertainty.

And yet, in His mercy, God didn't walk away when I questioned Him. He didn't silence me when I wept or even when I shook my fist. Instead, He began planting seeds of hope that maybe different wouldn't mean worse. That maybe it could even mean beautiful.

What I didn't realize was that this season of uncertainty was preparing me for more unknowns to come. The unraveling wasn't over. As I adjusted to life as a single mom, grieving not just a marriage but a vision for the future, another unexpected shift began to stir.

Walking away from a long and meaningful career didn't feel brave—it felt scary and disorienting. Though it was a choice, it also felt like another loss. Another stripping away of my identity. I missed the rhythm of the school year, the familiar faces, and the clear sense of purpose. For a while, though I knew I wanted to write, the way forward seemed unclear. I kept asking, *What now?*

---

23 Silvious, Jan. *Courage for the Unknown Season: Navigating What's Next with Confidence and Hope.* Thomas Nelson, 2017.

But answers didn't come right away. Just the same gentle invitation: *Keep walking. Keep trusting. Keep sowing.*

Not long after stepping away from teaching, I was invited to contribute a chapter to a collaborative book about the holidays. It wasn't a huge opportunity—it was just one chapter—but it gave me space to write about how divorce had changed the way my son and I celebrated. Reflecting on unmet expectations and how we made space for joy anyway felt surprisingly healing. It wasn't a great theological work or a bestseller. But something stirred as I shared my story. For the first time, I felt the soil shift. I wasn't just stepping out of the classroom. I was stepping into a calling.

In some of my most uncertain seasons, my trust in the Lord grew, but not because I had answers. It grew because I kept moving forward, one small, trembling step at a time. Obedience often comes before clarity. We want to see the full path before we take the first step, but faith isn't built like that. Faith doesn't mean we're fearless. It means we move anyway, trusting the One who holds the future. God doesn't grow our faith through perfectly laid-out plans—He grows it in the process.

Unknown seasons can be scary, yes. You may not see more than the one step in front of you. But here's the promise: God goes with you. And He makes a way.

I know what it's like to carry pain so heavy, it feels almost impossible to hope again. For a long time, I buried those wounds deep, convinced they were too broken, too hardened for God to redeem. But slowly, over time, God began to till the soil of my heart—not all at once, but with gentle, patient hands. He came with kindness, softening what I had sealed off, bringing life to the places I thought were beyond repair.

It's a paradox, isn't it? The same soil that once felt unyielding becomes the very place where something transformational begins to grow. The seeds of righteousness—the seeds of truth, grace, and love—start to take root, and slowly but surely, they push through the cracks of our once-hardened hearts.

For years, I held onto seeds of shame, self-doubt, and insecurity, letting them burrow deep into my heart. They shaped how I saw myself and whispered lies about my worth. But through therapy, prayer, and time in God's Word, I've come to break up the lies and hardened soil of self-rejection to receive God's truth.

Brennan Manning reminds us: "If we continue to view ourselves as moral lepers and spiritual failures, if our lives are shadowed by low self-esteem, shame, remorse, unhealthy guilt, and self-hatred, we reject the teaching of Jesus and cling to our negative self-image."[24]

Ouch. That one stings a bit, doesn't it? I don't know about you, but I never want to be known as someone who rejects the teaching of Jesus. Yet as hard as it may be to hear, Manning's statement is true. If we truly trust and believe God, that includes believing who He says we are—not the lies we've allowed to take root.

It means surrendering the seeds of shame and replacing them with seeds of righteousness: truth, hope, love, and healing.

God not only refines us; He invites us to participate in new growth. But first, He calls us to prepare the soil of our hearts: "Break up your unplowed ground, and do not sow among thorns" (Jeremiah 4:3, NIV). In other words, don't keep planting the seeds of truth in ground still choked by shame, fear, or bitterness. Let

---

24 Manning, Brennan. *Abba's Child: The Cry of the Heart for Intimate Belonging.* NavPress, 2002.

God expose and uproot what's been crowding out His voice, so His truth can actually grow.

Henri Nouwen's words speak to this holy invitation:

> *Listening to that voice with great inner attentiveness, I hear at my center words that say: 'I have called you by name from the very beginning. You are mine and I am yours... Wherever you go, I go with you, and wherever you rest, I keep watch. I will give you food that will satisfy all your hunger and drink that will quench all your thirst. I will not hide my face from you.'*[25]

These are not new promises—they are ancient and enduring. They've been whispered in the dark, clung to in the wilderness, and sung by generations who dared to dwell in God's presence. What Nouwen names so tenderly, the psalmist proclaims with confidence: "Whoever dwells in the shelter of the Most High will rest in the shadow of the Almighty. I will say of the Lord, 'He is my refuge and my fortress, my God, in whom I trust'" (Psalm 91:1, NIV).

Here's the truth: God's love is the safe place where we begin again. It's the shelter where our broken pieces are gathered. And from that place of security, He begins the rebuilding.

Restoration doesn't come from striving. It comes from abiding. It comes from faithfully following the One who's already at work beneath the surface.

Pause for a moment, and ask yourself: What seeds is God inviting me to plant in this season? Seeds of trust? Seeds of courage?

---

25 Nouwen, Henri J.M. *Life of the Beloved: Spiritual Living in a Secular World,* Crossroad Publishing Company, 2002, pp. 30–31.

Seeds of grace? The soil may feel dry or uncertain, but He's already preparing it. All He asks is that we plant what He provides.

So keep tending the soil. Keep planting in faith. Even when the ground looks barren, even when nothing seems to be breaking through, trust this: growth is still happening. The same God who plants the seeds is also the One who brings the harvest—in His time, in His way, and often in the very places we thought were beyond repair.

You are not just surviving a season.
You are being rooted.
You are growing.

Restoration Within Reach

More often than not, restoration begins closer than we realize. It's not always about striving or searching for something "out there." Sometimes, it's about uncovering what's been there all along, what God has already placed near us, waiting to be discovered.

Recently, I was watching a story about The Alamo on *Good Morning America*. They were finally beginning the long-overdue restoration of its weathered limestone walls. But for years, the process had been stalled. Why? Because to preserve its integrity, they needed limestone from the *original* source. The trouble was, no one knew where that was. Then, almost miraculously, construction crews uncovered a deposit near the San Antonio Zoo, just three miles away. It was a perfect match. The material they needed to rebuild had been right there all along.

That hidden deposit near the zoo had been there—waiting. Not lost. Just buried. And maybe that's true for you, too. Maybe what you need to begin rebuilding isn't somewhere far off. Maybe it's already been planted inside of you by the hand of God, waiting for its time to rise.

When I think about that limestone, I can't help but wonder how many parts of my healing were quietly waiting inside me, too. Not missing—just waiting to be seen. The courage to write. The truth about my identity in Christ. The resilience I didn't know I had. They weren't gone. They were simply waiting for me to return to the Source.

Isn't that just like our own restoration stories? We spend so much time searching for healing in all the wrong places, trying to patch ourselves up with quick fixes or cover the cracks with performance, perfection, or distraction. We reach for new jobs, new relationships, new distractions, hoping they will fill the hollow places inside us. But true restoration doesn't come from something new and shiny. It comes from returning to what's original. What's true. What was there from the beginning.

God doesn't ask us to manufacture healing from scratch. He invites us back to Himself—to the Source. To the One who formed us and knows exactly what we need to be made whole again.

Often, the process of restoration isn't flashy or fast. It's slow and meaningful. It looks like pausing long enough to listen. Like letting go of the frantic search for answers and learning instead to receive. Sometimes it looks like picking up an old truth we've forgotten: *You are still loved. You are still seen. You are not too far gone.*

> *The Lord will guide you always;*
> *he will satisfy your needs in a sun-scorched land*
> *and will strengthen your frame.*

You will be like a well-watered garden,
like a spring whose waters never fail.
(Isaiah 58:11, NIV)

God supplies the nourishment. But just like the land, we have to make space to receive it. The soil of our hearts must be open—willing to be tilled, softened, and made ready for new growth.

Restoration always comes from something old and something new. A house that is restored with its time-tested frame endures while new beams and fresh paint breathe life into every room. The Alamo's weathered walls, too, will soon welcome limestone quarried from the original source—ancient stone meeting modern hands. And a seed? It's the perfect illustration: a tiny remnant of what once was, holding within it the blueprint of what will be. God doesn't just discard the old; He folds it into the new, using every scar and story as scaffolding for fresh growth.

The Seeds We Sow

What we plant will grow—eventually. And not just in the soil of our lives, but in the lives of those around us. Hosea says, "Sow righteousness for yourselves..." (Hosea 10:12, NIV). Not righteousness for show. Not righteousness to earn favor. But righteousness that reflects a heart rooted in God.

When Hosea told the people to "sow righteousness," it was a call to repentance and renewal. A call to return to the One who could make their hearts whole again. And it's the same invitation God extends to us: Come back. Clear the ground. Plant in faith.

We sow righteousness when we choose grace over gossip. When we extend kindness instead of keeping score. When we speak truth gently, not to be right, but to reflect Christ. We sow righteousness when we choose peace instead of sarcasm and mercy instead of resentment. When we show up in obedience, even when the outcome feels invisible. When we do the right thing because it's *right*, not because it's immediately rewarding.

And that's hard sometimes. Because let's be honest. There's no standing ovation for biting your tongue when you could have been proven right. No applause for choosing prayer over panic. No award for apologizing first or forgiving again.

But these are the quiet choices that shape a holy life.

They are the seeds that bloom into something eternal.

Sowing righteousness doesn't mean you get it all right. It just means you're aligning your planting with God's heart. And in time—sometimes in surprising ways—He brings the harvest.

So if sowing righteousness feels like a slow, silent effort, and if you wonder whether it's worth it, take heart. When your feet feel stuck in the mud, and the next step is hidden in shadows, remember: God is near. He is whispering, "*I am with you. I will make a way. I will restore what has been lost.*"

This is the call to begin again. Not with your own strength, but with His. To trust that beneath the ashes, beneath the mess, God is planting seeds of righteousness, seeds of hope, seeds of life that will one day bear the fruit of His unfailing love.

May you dare to plant even when the soil feels dry. May you trust the silence as much as the voice. May your roots grow deep in the truth of who you are, and may the harvest surprise you with joy.

Beauty in BLOOM

B–Believe It

- Breaking ground isn't easy. It's disruptive, painful, and vulnerable. But it's also where restoration begins.
- God doesn't need you to have the whole plan. He just asks you to keep moving in faith.

L–Linger

- "Sow righteousness for yourselves, reap the fruit of unfailing love, and break up your unplowed ground; for it is time to seek the Lord, until he comes and showers his righteousness on you" (Hosea 10:12, NIV).

O–Observe

- Where do you feel stuck or hardened right now spiritually, emotionally, or physically?
- Where is God calling you to dig deeper?
- What might growth require in this season?

O–Offer Prayer

God,
I come to You with a heart that's been through fire,
a soul weathered by storms,
and soil worn and weary.
And still—here I am, ready to begin again.
I know You're not finished with me.
You don't discard scorched ground. You restore it.
You don't waste the dark seasons. You prepare the soil.
Plant in me seeds of truth—
that I am loved, chosen, seen, and called.

May this new season be rooted in righteousness,
nourished by grace,
and covered in Your faithfulness.
In Jesus' name, Amen.

M–Magnify

- If you could plant something new—a habit, a mindset, a dream—what would it be? How will you tend to it?
- Commit Hosea 10:12 or Joshua 1:9 to memory. Let one become a spiritual anchor.

8

Waiting for the Ashes to Bloom
Trusting God in the Transformation

"You have to dare to trust that the pain you think
will kill you can be a pain that heals you."
—Henri J.M. Nouwen[26]

Among the Ashes

The air was muggy and thick as I stood along the banks of the Cumberland River, watching fireworks paint the night sky in bursts of red, white, and blue. It was Independence Day, and thousands of us had gathered downtown for the celebration. Each firework exploded with a thud I could feel in my chest.

---

26 Nouwen, Henri J.M. *The Inner Voice of Love: A Journey Through Anguish to Freedom.* Doubleday, 1996.

The sky was a masterpiece of light and sound, as strangers stood side by side, cheering together under a canopy of stars and sparks. The symphony played as the fireworks burst to life in rhythm with the music. It was one of those collective moments that felt almost magical.

But as the show went on, I noticed something else—something heavier. A cloud of gray ash drifted slowly across the river, silent reminders of the bursts that came before. Within minutes, the ash began to settle on everything—our clothes, our skin, our hair. Some people brushed it off. Others just let it fall. I paused as I brushed some from my shoulder, because this ash carried meaning. A residue of beauty spent. A remnant of celebration turned quiet.

The thing about ashes is they don't show up unless something has burned. Sometimes it was a good fire—a dream, a celebration, a mountaintop moment. But even those leave residue. And sometimes, we grieve what was good because it ended.

The ash on my shoulders didn't weigh much, but it made me think about the invisible weight we all carry—the kind that doesn't fall in dramatic bursts but settles quietly over time. Ashes from what once was. Hopes that burst bright and then burned out. Moments of joy that left behind an ache we didn't see coming. Grief we didn't ask for but couldn't ignore.

We all carry ashes. Some of us try to brush them off, pretending they're not there. Others wear them like a second skin, unsure how to move forward with the weight of what's been lost. Sometimes, we don't even realize how heavy it's become until we try to move forward and feel stuck.

Ash has a way of clinging to us. Not just physically, but spiritually. It marks what used to be, and it reminds us of the space between what we hoped for and what actually happened.

Fire Followers

I sat in the chair at the hair salon and told my stylist, "I am afraid I am going to be an old maid with eighty cats…alone the rest of my life. I've not been attracted to anyone since my divorce." She and I shared a good laugh about it. Little did we know that very night God would bring a handsome man from Arizona to the same gathering I was attending.

One of my students' parents was hosting a welcome party for a group of authors attending the writing conference he had organized. Sometime earlier in the week, this parent popped into my classroom and, clearly with little faith in my social life, asked, "What are you doing Friday night? Nothing, right? You're coming to my house for a party." A bit taken aback by his assumption I'd have no plans, I entertained the idea as part of a girls' night out with two of the other teachers he'd invited, who also happened to be two of my close friends.

Knowing the party was for authors of suspense and thriller novels, my friends and I assumed we'd be entering a crowd in which we'd feel like fish out of water, and, no offense, but likely that those in attendance weren't going to be our kind of people. Not bad. Just different. With this in mind, we made a plan to stay at the party for all of fifteen minutes, then out for a fun girls' night of dinner and games. We walked up the brick path to the front porch. We hesitantly entered the house to find people milling about, making small talk, and peering somewhat subtly at Jeffrey Deaver, a famous thriller writer, who also happened to be in attendance. This solidified our idea that we weren't really going to fit in with this crowd.

Until…a moment I'll never forget. I walked down the steps after being given a full tour of the house by my student, and there *he* stood by the front door. Dark hair, button-down shirt with a jacket, and such a handsome face with piercing eyes that still make my heart melt when he looks at me. So much for thinking I'd be an old maid with eighty cats. Seeing this dream of a man cured that in a heartbeat.

After getting past the giggles and nervousness with my friends, like middle school girls deciding whether or not to talk to the cute guy at a dance, the host of the party caught wind of what we were discussing and made an introduction. I can't tell you what I said that night, but I'm pretty sure I was a bumbling mess. This exquisite man and I sat and talked with my friends for three hours. So long that we ended up being the last ones at the party and drove him back to his hotel.

I never would have imagined that this is how I would meet the man God had been preparing me for, and him for me.

While there's much more to our story, suffice it to say, we fell in love hard and fast (and quickly racked up frequent flier miles). For just over seven years, my husband and I dated long distance—he in Phoenix, me in Nashville. As much as I would have loved to have run off to Vegas and marry this man at any point during our dating years, God knew better. He was still molding and shaping us for one another, so the beauty of a life together could be better than we could imagine.

We often joke that we're yin and yang in more ways than one, and that contrast was never more apparent than when we'd fly between our cities.

The first time I drove across I-10 in Arizona, I was struck by the landscape. Jagged mountains stretched across a shockingly blue sky—a kind of blue that felt deeper somehow than anything I'd seen before. But beneath that vast sky, the land lay dry and cracked, the valleys wide and worn and weary with dust. It was beautiful in its own way.

The desert wasn't empty. It was preparing me to see beauty differently.

Each time I came home to Tennessee, it was as if the whole world had suddenly turned Technicolor. Trees towered in vibrant green, rolling hills, and everything seemed to buzz with life. I'd never noticed it before, not really. But after the desert, the lushness felt extravagant.

Still, Arizona had its own kind of wild beauty. One day, as we drove along the highway, I looked out the window and said, "I love the wildflowers spread along the roadside."

He nodded in agreement, "Without the flowers, it'd look barren. Depressing even."

He was right. Those little blooms felt like confetti tossed by hope itself. Bright, defiant, almost celebratory. They pushed up through dry, cracked earth with boldness, unbothered by the heat or the hard conditions. Like they'd heard the forecast and decided to bloom anyway.

But it made me wonder: what about when the ground isn't just dry but scorched? What about when everything has burned?

How do ashes bloom?

My heart was overwhelmed to discover the beautiful parallels between how ashes bloom in nature and how God prepares our lives for beauty to bloom, even in spite of the ashes.

Ashes are what's left when something has ended—what's been consumed, destroyed, or broken down. They feel final. But in both nature and faith, ashes don't always mean it's over. Sometimes, they're the starting point.

In nature, after a wildfire, everything seems lost. The land is blackened, hushed, lifeless. But underneath, something remarkable is happening. Did you know some seeds actually require fire to sprout? These "fire followers" are wildflowers whose seeds lie dormant under the ground, sometimes even for decades before they bloom. Mary Potter Kerns explains:

> *After a fire, many of these 'fire-flowers' that have been dormant for decades or more, will burst into bloom in mass, in amazing displays of color, blanketing the charred landscape. It feels like they are answering the devastation of the wildfire with a fiery passion of their own, bursting forth from the dirt in a riot of color, trumpeting a new cycle of life with almost unbelievable beauty.[27]*

The ash enriches the soil, and in time, new life begins to rise. What looked like ruin was really the beginning of renewal.

But not all growth is visible right away. Sometimes we want proof that something is changing, something is blooming. But the most important growth often happens beneath the surface, in silence and stillness. That can feel frustrating, even defeating. But God often does His most sacred work in the hidden places. Our job isn't to force fruit to appear; it's to stay rooted in Him.

---

27 Kerns, Mary Potter. "Born of Fire." *The Flowers Are Speaking*, 11 Jan. 2023, https://theflowersarespeaking.com/2023/01/11/born-of-fire/. Accessed 27 January 2025.

Henri Nouwen writes, "You have to trust that the deeper you live your life with Me [God], the more fruitful it will be, even though you may not always see that fruit."[28]

When you're in a season of silence or waiting, when the soil looks bare and the fire still smolders, remember this: just because you don't see the fruit doesn't mean it's not growing. The roots are going deep. The soil is being nourished. The bloom will come, in God's time, and it will be worth the wait.

The ashes of grief, loss, heartbreak, shame—they feel heavy. Final. But God doesn't let our devastation go to waste. In the deep work of healing and grace, He brings beauty out of what we thought was beyond repair. Out of the ruins, He cultivates compassion, wisdom, resilience, and purpose. He rebuilds, reshapes, redeems.

Isaiah tells us that God gives "...a crown of beauty instead of ashes..." (Isaiah 61:3, NIV). He doesn't just sweep up the ruins. He transforms them. He trades our despair for joy, our mourning for dancing, our ashes for something radiant.

So how do ashes bloom?

They bloom when we trust that what we've lost is not lost on God.

They bloom when grace soaks into the scorched places.

They bloom when we dare—sometimes trembling—to hope again.

---

28   Nouwen, Henri J.M. *The Inner Voice of Love: A Journey Through Anguish to Freedom.* Doubleday, 1996, p. 70.

Becoming a Fire Follower

Growth and restoration don't happen all at once. They require waiting. The kind that tests your trust and feels like nothing is happening when everything actually is.

For the land, the aftermath of fire begins with quiet work—ashes and charcoal sinking in, enriching the soil with nutrients. Nothing looks different at first. But over time, seeds long dormant awaken, organic life returns, and what once looked dead begins to live again. Trees stretch upward. Roots settle deep. Balance and beauty slowly find their way back.

And just as scorched earth heals in stages, so did I. My own recovery mirrored that rhythm: slow, uneven, sacred. Waiting wasn't wasted. It was part of the work.

Immediately: I clung to God's Word like oxygen. The Psalms became a lifeline, devotionals like *Jesus Calling* spoke directly into my fear and fatigue, and the voices of family and close friends formed a protective circle around my broken heart. I was too raw to process anything fully, but I could still *breathe*. That was enough.

In the Weeks and Months that Followed: Provision arrived like rain in a desert—unexpected, generous, and always just in time. Jobs that allowed me to stay close to my son. Financial gifts we hadn't asked for. Little mercies that felt like God whispering, *I see you.* I began therapy and the patient work of unearthing the deeper pain that had been buried beneath all my striving.

In the First Year: My son and I moved into an apartment of our own. It wasn't just a change of address; it felt like planting something new. Each box unpacked was an act of acceptance, each room a declaration: *We are still growing.* It was stability, yes, but also a fragile kind of courage.

In the Years that Followed: The deeper work took root. Forgiveness and shame don't lift easily; they cling. But little by little, God dug into the hard places. He exposed what I'd buried—anger, insecurity, sorrow—and began the long, worthy process of making me whole. Some healing came like a sudden bloom; other pieces only revealed themselves in hindsight.

Each season layered healing upon healing. The process wasn't linear, but it was faithful. Through every stumble and stillness, God met me right where I was, patiently rewriting the story I thought was finished. And over time, I saw something surprising take root: not just survival, not just recovery...but renewal.

God doesn't just restore what was lost in the fire. He brings forth blooms that could only grow *because* of it.

It's a hard truth to hold when the flames are still fresh—when we're standing in the ashes of a life we didn't choose. But the God we serve is not merely a restorer. He is the Creator of holy new things. As Pope Francis said, "Although the life of a person is a land full of thorns and weeds, there is always a space in which the good seed can grow. You have to trust God."[29]

Just like fire-followers—those wildflowers that rise from scorched soil—there are parts of us that don't awaken until after the devastation. They need the heat. The breaking. The clearing.

God doesn't just give back what was taken. He gives us what we never imagined possible: deeper joy, unexpected peace, stronger roots, and beauty that only makes sense in the light of what we've walked through.

That's the mystery of grace.

---

29 Francis, Pope. *A Big Heart Open to God: A Conversation with Pope Francis.* Interview by Antonio Spadaro, HarperOne, 2013.

God doesn't just bring life from ashes. He untangles what we thought was ruined. The beauty was never lost. It was just waiting to be set free.

Grace in the Untangling

I unzipped my travel bag and stared at the chaos I'd accidentally created—a hopeless knot of earrings and necklaces twisted tight like a tiny web of frustration. I sighed, angry at myself for not packing more carefully, but also… tired. Tired of trying to fix things. Tired of holding messes in my hands and not knowing where to start.

It felt like more than jewelry. It felt like a mirror. In that moment, God was using this mess to teach me that I often try to untangle the mess of my life by my own hands and my own power.

A year passed without any further attempts to untangle the mess of jewelry, but just as I was preparing to count it a loss and throw it away, I decided to give it one more try. This time, instead of focusing on the impossibility of the task or the overwhelming desire to force the chains apart with a quick, strong pull, I began to slowly and gently focus on one chain at a time. Much to my surprise, one by one, the knots started to loosen. The chains began to move more freely, and the mess became untangled. The jewelry's beauty and purpose were now restored.

As I sat looking at the individual pieces, I was reminded that we must bring our messes and become undone before God, for only His hands, His love, His light can make us beautiful. What God was teaching me even a year prior resurfaced as a lesson I needed once again.

Amidst the chains of past hurts and unforgiveness, I sat overwhelmed by the task at hand. I sat wallowing in pride, focusing on what seemed impossible—forgiving someone who had intentionally hurt me. In truth, trying to work toward forgiveness on my own only made me more of a tangled mess, easily knotted up by bitterness and even hate. Through this wad of jewelry on my nightstand, I was reminded that I must loosen my grip, stop focusing on what seems impossible, open my hands, and release the tangled mess that is my heart to the God who can free me from the bondage of all sin, hurt, and unforgiveness. It is not by my power that the knots of sin may become undone, but by His power and grace alone.

God made it abundantly clear. Forgiveness would be key to my healing. It would take time, though. Time spent praying and listening to God. Ultimately, He didn't demand that I forgive those who hurt me. He invited me to forgive because He knew what carrying bitterness would cost me.

Forgiveness was a turning point in my healing journey, but your healing may require something else of you. Healing looks different for each of us, because it is layered. It's not just about releasing others; it's also about letting God restore *us*. At some point, healing becomes less about what happened to us and more about what God is doing *in* us. He's not just patching up wounds. He's redeeming the entire story.

As such, it takes time and tending for our wounds to give way to new beauty. Not because God is slow, but because some growth happens beneath the surface. We water with prayer, nourish with rest, and keep showing up—even when the soil feels dry.

What is God doing in your heart? What is God showing you that you need to untangle before you can bloom? What other sacred steps might He be calling you into so you can find healing?

Sometimes healing means asking, "Why did I respond that way?" or "What have I been carrying that doesn't belong to me?" When we understand the patterns we've been living in, we're more equipped to live out of God's truth.

Healing often requires boundaries—saying no without guilt, stepping back from harmful people, or simply creating space to breathe. Boundaries aren't walls to keep people out; they're gates to guard what's growing inside.

Maybe God is asking you to surrender control and trust Him. There comes a moment when we realize: *I can't fix this.* And maybe that's the invitation—to stop striving and start surrendering. To trust that God is not only able to heal, but deeply *wants* to.

Our hearts don't heal on command. We can't rush what God is still unraveling. We can't force freedom when we're still learning to release. For me, that process unfolded slowly.

When the Waiting Turns to Release

It took five years.

It took five years to come to a place of forgiving her—the other woman.

It took five years for me to hear God say, "She is also My child. Also loved. Also forgiven."

But before I could accept that, I wrestled with God. *"How am I supposed to forgive someone who wrecked my life?"* I remember thinking, *"She knew what she was doing. She knew my son and me, and she still did it anyway. How am I supposed to let this go?"* The bitterness felt justified—almost necessary. Forgiveness felt like letting her off the hook, like giving up the last bit of power I had left.

It took five years for me to write a letter, releasing the hurt, pain, and anger I had harbored in my heart.

As a believer and one prone to a mindset of shame, I could look back on that time and shame myself for not forgiving her (or him) sooner. But instead, I see that God was using that time, those five years, to stretch me, teach me, and help me come to a place I could fully surrender all to Him and truly forgive. Not just in word, but in action, and most importantly, in my heart. He had been untangling the roots of anger and bitterness within me.

I picked up my pen and stared at the blank page for what felt like forever. *"What am I even supposed to say? What if this doesn't bring peace?"* The thought of putting my heart into words felt risky, exposing. Yet somehow, I knew it was time. Not because I felt ready—but because I trusted God was.

And so, after five years, I wrote and sent this letter:

> *Dear xxxxxx,*
>
> *I have written this letter many times. In honesty, the message has not always been the one I wish to share with you today. I have had varying degrees of emotions and feelings throughout my process these past several years, and in dealing with the ongoing ramifications of how life has unfolded. And whether or not you need or want to hear this from me, I know that it is part of my own closure in expressing these truths, so I hope you'll read on...*
>
> *First, **you are loved**. I do not know what led to your affair years ago, but I can imagine that the desire to feel and be loved and cherished was somehow a part of that. What I pray you know is that **you are loved by One***

who will never stop loving you…no matter what.
There is no one who can love us like Jesus. I pray that it is in Him that you find your value, worth, and beauty.

Secondly, **I forgive you.** *I couldn't always say that, but in my own process from grieving to growth through grace, I have come to that place. More importantly, I hope you know the depth of God's forgiveness and have been able to experience His mercy, grace, and restoration to its full extent.*

Lastly, **I am praying for you.** *My hope is that you have come to a place of peace and that God will use your story (and mine) to help others know His great love and redemption.*

Sincerely,

Sarah

"[May] the Lord bless you and keep you; The Lord make his face shine upon you, and be gracious unto you; [May] the Lord lift up His countenance upon you, and give you peace." —Numbers 6:24–26, ESV

Finally forgiving someone who had been at the root of such pain in my life, while it was hopefully healing to her as well, was most freeing to me. I felt a weight lifted from my soul.

Maybe you find yourself struggling to forgive.

Letting go of unforgiveness is rarely neat or easy. It's one of those brave, gritty acts of obedience that may not bring instant relief, but it opens wide the door for God's healing to pour in. Forgiveness is not about excusing what happened. It's about refusing to let bitterness be the narrator of your story.

Before you can release unforgiveness, you have to face what happened and admit how it hurt you. Not sugarcoating it. Not brushing it off. Just telling the truth. God isn't asking you to pretend it didn't hurt. He's inviting you to bring the real, raw version of your pain to Him.

Letting go of unforgiveness may feel like a slow unraveling, but every choice to release it makes room for something new: healing, peace, freedom. And you don't have to do it alone. God walks every step with you, patient and kind, never rushing the process, but always faithful to complete what He's begun in you.

Forgiveness is a vital part of healing, but it's not the only part. Forgiveness loosens the hold of what hurt us, softens the soil of bitterness, and prepares our hearts for what God wants to grow next. Beauty begins to bloom in the fields of forgiveness, but healing often grows across many landscapes.

Sometimes what God asks us to release in the waiting isn't a person. Sometimes it's control. Or expectations. Or the timeline we thought our healing should follow. Maybe it's shame you've carried too long. Or the fear that if you stop striving, you'll start sinking.

So let me ask you: What is God inviting you to loosen your grip on in this season? What burden have you been carrying that He never asked you to hold? Take a moment to name it. Write it down. Offer it to Him—not because you're done with it, but because He can do something with it. Something redemptive. Something beautiful.

Where Ashes Begin to Bloom

It's one thing to talk about restoration in hindsight—when healing has taken root, the pieces are slowly coming back together, and the story starts to make sense again. But what about the in-between? What about when the fire has just swept through, and all you can see is what's been lost?

Sometimes, before anything can grow, the ground must be scorched. And in those moments when the flames feel overwhelming, it helps to remember: God is not absent from the fire. He's right there in it with us. As Timothy Keller writes in *Walking with God through Pain and Suffering*, "Suffering can refine us rather than destroy us because God himself walks with us in the fire."[30] His presence changes everything. What might consume us instead becomes the very place where He reshapes and restores.

It's a hard thing to grasp, but fire doesn't just destroy; it transforms. It refines. And in the spiritual life, it often reveals what's been hidden and purifies what's been tainted. What the enemy meant to burn down, God can use to light the way forward.

I think back to the fire-followers I mentioned earlier—those bold little wildflowers that lie dormant in the dirt for years, just waiting for the right conditions. They don't bloom in spite of the fire—they bloom because of it. They need the heat, the clearing, the ash. What looks like devastation is actually what wakes them up.

And I wonder...what if parts of our soul are like that, too?

What if there are pieces of hope, courage, compassion, and purpose lying dormant inside of you, waiting for the heat to come, so they can bloom?

It's hard to believe in new beginnings when all we feel is grief or shame or heartbreak. But friend, hear me: you're not standing

---

30   Keller, Timothy. *Walking with God Through Pain and Suffering*. Riverhead Books, 2013.

in a wasteland. You're standing on sacred ground. God is doing something deep beneath the surface. Even if you don't see it yet—even if it feels like nothing is changing—the roots are growing.

Healing comes slowly. And sometimes the most meaningful transformation happens while everything above the surface still looks barren. Isaiah 43:19 doesn't promise that we'll always see the new thing right away. It reminds us that God is doing something, whether we perceive it or not. I still don't always see clearly. But I've learned to look with faith instead of fear. To trust that what God plants in scorched soil will bloom in His time, even if I can't see it yet.

So if you're in that in-between place where the fire has passed but the landscape still feels bare, I want to gently remind you: *new life is already underway.* It might not look like much yet. It might not feel like healing. But God's not asking you to rush the bloom. He's inviting you to walk with Him in it. He's inviting you to trust the process, to walk with Him in the slow and sacred in-between.

Sometimes the first step toward beauty is simply learning to notice where He's already planting seeds. Sometimes, it's taking time to look for the beauty already in bloom.

Beauty in BLOOM

B–Believe It

- God brings forth blooms that could only grow because of the fire.
- Before you can release unforgiveness, you have to face what happened and admit how it hurt you.
- Forgiveness is not about excusing what happened. It's about refusing to let bitterness be the narrator of your story.

L–Linger

- Spend a few quiet minutes with Isaiah 43:18–19.
- Ask yourself: *What pain might God be inviting me to release so He can make space for something new?*

O–Observe

- Where does your heart feel scorched or silent?
- What hints of hope—small "fire followers"—are beginning to rise?
- What new life are you still waiting for?
- Even if you can't see it yet, what do you *sense* God is nurturing below the surface?

O–Offer Prayer

Lord,

I'm still standing in the ashes, and honestly, I don't see much blooming yet. But I believe You're here, working beneath the surface, even when I can't feel it.

Help me trust You with this scorched soil.

Grow something beautiful where it feels like nothing could ever grow again.

I'll wait here, with open hands, believing You're not done.

In Jesus' name, Amen.

M–Magnify

- Take time to trace your healing journey. Sometimes, growth isn't obvious until you look back and name it.
  - Immediately: What signs of hope, provision, or presence came first?
  - Weeks/Months: What new opportunities or healing began?
  - Year: What lasting shifts occurred?
  - Years Later: What transformation can you see now?

What the enemy tried to burn down, God is using to light your way forward.

What once felt like devastation is now hallowed ground—where beauty dares to bloom.

9

In Bloom

Becoming Who You Were Always Meant to Be

"Sometimes when you're in a dark place you think you've been buried, but actually you've been planted."
—Christine Caine[31]

Flourish Through Fire

I've never seen the redwoods, but they fascinate me. Redwoods are majestic, towering, and ancient. Some have stood for over two thousand years, reaching heights of more than 300 feet. But what's most surprising about these giants isn't their size—it's their relationship with fire.

Redwoods don't just survive fire.

They flourish because of it.

---

31 Caine, Christine. *Undaunted: Daring to Do What God Calls You to Do.* Zondervan, 2012.

Their bark is incredibly thick, almost spongy, with a natural fire-resistant quality. It insulates the tree's core during even the most intense wildfires. But here's where it gets even more fascinating: many redwood cones won't release their seeds unless exposed to extreme heat. The fire actually triggers new life. It clears the forest floor of competing underbrush, making way for sunlight to reach the soil. In the aftermath of what looks like devastation… growth begins.

Maybe that's where you are right now: singed by sorrow, standing among ashes, unsure if anything beautiful could grow in this place again. Maybe you're wondering if the fire will ever end. If anything good could possibly come from what's been lost. You're not alone, friend—and you're not without hope. If that's you, I want to gently whisper this truth:

You were made to flourish through fire.

Not in spite of it. Not after it's over. *Through* it.

What if this isn't just a fire to survive, but a place where lasting beauty is being forged? The Spirit is with you in the flames, shaping a faith that's deeper, stronger, and built to endure.

The presence of fire in your story isn't proof that God has abandoned you. It may actually be the very thing He's using to prepare you for deeper growth. As Christine Caine wisely said, "Sometimes when you're in a dark place you think you've been buried, but actually you've been planted."[32] What feels like the end might actually be the beginning of something new. Buried things aren't always lost; sometimes they're being positioned for growth.

---

32 Caine, Christine. *Undaunted: Daring to Do What God Calls You to Do*. Zondervan, 2012.

When life feels dark, desolate, or dormant, God may be doing His most transformative work beneath the surface.

As we are reminded in the book of Romans, "And we know that in all things God works for the good of those who love Him, who have been called according to His purpose" (Romans 8:28, NIV).

Like the redwoods, you're more resilient than you feel. And under the surface, something is stirring. New life. Fresh hope. Unseen strength.

So don't fear the fire.

God is in it, and He's not finished with your story yet. What was scorched has become redemptive. What once seemed like loss led to unexpected beauty.

The beauty God brings from ashes isn't always immediate, and it rarely looks like what we expected. Sometimes, it begins slowly, like trust being rebuilt, joy returning in fragments, or the steady sense that you are not forgotten. And then, sometimes, it surprises you completely. Just when I had made peace with the wilderness, God began writing a new chapter—one that would bloom not in spite of the fire, but right in the middle of scorched ground. That's how I found myself stepping into a story I never could have scripted: a wedding in the wilderness.

A Wedding in the Wilderness

My husband and I had both been through painful divorces. We both carried wounds with us into the relationship. But we were both committed to ensuring our marriage would be different than what we had experienced. God gave us a strong foundation of trust, the gift of time to truly get to know one another on a deeper, spiritual level, and a shared vision for what our future together would be like.

It wasn't until I sat down to begin writing this book that I saw the incredible full-circle beauty from ashes God had given us.

Once we were engaged, we decided to have a small family wedding. We rented a place in Gatlinburg, Tennessee, with a living room that had an incredible, wall-length view of the expansive mountains spread across the horizon. My dad became an ordained minister just so he could officiate the ceremony, and all the plans were set.

Then Gatlinburg was on fire. Literally.

It had been devastated by wildfires, and some were still burning just a month before we were to get married. The owners reassured us that the home we rented was safe to visit, so we stuck with our plan.

As we drove slowly up the side of the mountain, we were surrounded by ash from trees knocked over and scorched. Complete homes had burned to their foundation, leaving wide gaps across the landscape. I couldn't believe my eyes. It was truly devastating. Looking out the window as we drove past the house next door to the one we rented for our wedding, we were shocked and saddened to see that there was nothing left except for a concrete parking pad.

My heart beat wildly in my chest, unsure of what we would find when we arrived at the rental home. But God had already prepared this place—a space for something new and beautiful to begin.

Though the landscape was charred, even desolate in places, the home we'd reserved still stood, untouched by the fire that had caused so much damage. This, to me, was a symbol of God's provision and sovereignty.

The fact that our wedding stood on fire-scorched ground wasn't just poetic—it was prophetic. God was showing me, right there in the wilderness, that He truly does restore what's been broken. Not just with a new beginning, but with His presence woven through every chapter that followed.

We were in the literal wilderness. Experiencing a new beginning. A wedding, a marriage, was rising from charred ground. God made a way in the wilderness. In the very place where all had burned to the ground, right there in the middle of the ashes, He gave us beauty. A forever marriage. But not just a different marriage, one *better than before.*

It was just as He said in Isaiah: "See, I am doing a new thing! Now it springs up; do you not perceive it? I am making a way in the wilderness and streams in the wasteland" (Isaiah 43:19, NIV).

The Greek word for "new" in this verse is "chadash," meaning fresh, renewed, or restored. Not just different, but *better than before.*

When All Feels Burned

Much like the scorched mountainside after a wildfire, seasons of desolation can leave us feeling like hope has gone silent, like all that once was vibrant has been reduced to ash. The landscape of our lives feels stripped bare. But just as fire-prepared soil becomes the perfect place for redwood seeds to sprout, the broken places in our lives—the ones refined by fire—are often where grace takes deepest root.

Pain can prepare the soil.

As Paul tells us in Romans 5: "Not only so, but we also glory in our sufferings, because we know that suffering produces perseverance; perseverance, character; and character, hope. And hope does not put us to shame, because God's love has been poured out into our hearts through the Holy Spirit, who has been given to us" (Romans 5:3–5, NIV).

These aren't just poetic words; they're the anatomy of resilience.

- **Suffering**: It feels like the end, but it's the start of something holy.

- **Perseverance**: This isn't just white-knuckling our way through life. It's leaning into God's strength when ours runs dry. Perseverance isn't just surviving; it's becoming.

- **Character**: This is who we become in the fire. When we keep showing up, keep trusting, keep surrendering.

- **Hope**: The bloom. Not wishful thinking, but a deep confidence rooted in the love of God that will not let us go. Hope does not disappoint.

Tempting though it may be, don't skip the suffering. It is the seedbed of strength. As A.W. Tozer is often quoted, "It is doubtful whether God can bless a man greatly until He has hurt him deeply."[33] Whether or not he said it exactly that way, the point holds: blessings often emerge through brokenness.

Statements like this can make me pause and ask *How could a loving God allow such suffering? How could He let my life be stripped bare? Why would He use pain to produce strength?* The reality is that our suffering is not inflicted upon us by God; rather, He carries us through it and uses it for good.

---

33 Direct citation is not available. Concepts aligned with information found by A.W. Tozer.

I wrestled with this thought as I went through my divorce, and so many people told me God hadn't *caused* the infidelity or divorce, but that He *allowed* it. Easy to say. Easy to hear. Not so easy to accept. I had a tough time understanding why God would allow anything that resembled suffering when I had strived to follow Him so faithfully.

I have seen many around me go through unthinkable suffering. Relatives who have lost a child. A friend who struggled for years with infertility, and another whose adoption turned into a thing of nightmares. One friend lost a spouse to cancer, leaving her as a widow with a toddler. A family friend lost a daughter to suicide, and a student lost his mother in the same tragic way. Suffering, it seems, is something none of us escapes. But every once in a while, you meet someone whose story gives you a glimpse of God in the middle of it.

Hope in Bloom

Years ago, when my ex-husband worked for a Christian music publishing company in Nashville, I had the honor of meeting Nancy Guthrie—a Bible teacher, author, and speaker whose ministry has impacted thousands of people walking through grief and loss. Nancy and her husband had experienced the unimaginable: the loss of two children, Hope and Gabriel. Her honest wrestling with suffering, paired with unwavering trust in God's sovereignty, has made her a voice of deep comfort and credibility in the Christian community.

Her husband was my former husband's boss, and our paths crossed at a company Christmas party. While she would likely never remember our conversation, I will never forget it.

We stood in the corner as she held her five-month-old son, Gabriel, in her arms. Her daughter, Hope, had been born with a rare genetic disorder that caused her to pass away at only six months old. Now, she tenderly cared for Gabriel, knowing he, too, had the same disorder and would not live much longer.

My heart and mind could not comprehend the intense suffering she and her family had already endured, let alone knowing what they were facing with this precious child. Nancy was facing suffering in a way I was not sure I could survive.

Yet she had hope.

Not because of her own strength and will to push through, but because of her willingness to trust God in all circumstances.

In honesty, my human mind still cannot fully comprehend a response to the question of why God allows suffering. But I can speak of what I *do* know. God brings meaning and purpose to our suffering. In her book, *Holding Onto Hope*, a book she wrote while pregnant with Gabriel, Nancy Guthrie shares that being a child of God doesn't mean we won't suffer, rather:

> *It means no meaningless suffering. If God has allowed suffering into your life, it is for a purpose. A good purpose. A holy purpose.*
>
> *The world tells us to run from suffering, to avoid it at all costs, to cry out to heaven to take it away. Few of us would choose to suffer. Yet when we know that God has allowed suffering into our lives for a purpose, we can embrace it instead of running from it, and we can seek God in the midst of suffering. Accepting suffering drives us deeper in our devotion.*[34]

---

34 Guthrie, Nancy. *Holding Onto Hope*. Tyndale, 2002.

Her words echo what Paul wrote to the church in Corinth—a reminder that even our deepest trials are never wasted in the hands of God. "For our light and momentary troubles are achieving for us an eternal glory that far outweighs them all. So we fix our eyes not on what is seen, but on what is unseen..." (2 Corinthians 4:17-18, NIV). Suffering may feel all-consuming in the moment, but God assures us it is accomplishing something beyond what we can see. There is an unwavering hope being formed in us—a depth of character, of dependence, of devotion—that isn't possible without the fire. What we see now may look like ashes, but He is working in the unseen to bring beauty that lasts. The fire doesn't destroy. It clears the way.

In the months following my divorce, Nancy's *One Year Book of Hope* became my daily devotional. If this woman of faith who had suffered so greatly could think of a way to hold onto hope every day of the year, surely I could, too. Again, her words became like a salve for my wounds. Not because of what she said, but because of what God said and taught through her. The daily focus on hope helped me see God's goodness and faithfulness even in my heartache. It also helped restore and multiply my joy, even in the midst of my suffering.

Joy in suffering? That seems counterintuitive. But again, that's so like God. To take what we think and flip it on its head. Nancy put to words so beautifully what my soul experienced in those days as God began to help me bloom once again:

> To experience sorrow does not eliminate joy. In fact, I've come to think that sorrow actually deepens our capacity for joy—that as our lows are lower, so are our highs higher. Deep sorrow expands our ability to feel deeply... When joy surfaces, it allows us to see that deep beneath the

chaos and catastrophe is the strong current of confidence
that we can be content in the sovereign hands of God.
It's just not natural to experience profound joy in the
face of heartache. It is supernatural; it is spiritual. This
is the kind of joy God has for you. It is not produced by
the human spirit in response to pleasant circumstances,
but by the Holy Spirit in spite of difficult circumstances.
It is the very joy of Christ fulfilled in us.[35]

This truth, this word of hope, is rooted in both Nancy's personal experience and in God's Word. As Paul writes to the Corinthians, "Our hearts ache, but we always have joy. We are poor, but we give spiritual riches to others. We own nothing, and yet we have everything" (2 Cor. 6:10, NLT). The joy we carry, the hope that blooms, the strength we possess—it was always there, and it will forever be, no matter what we face.

It's the upside-down nature of the Kingdom—where sorrow and joy can coexist, where hope is not crushed by heartache but actually grows through it. Looking back, I can see how God was gently replanting joy in the soil of my grief, like a tender shoot pressing through the dirt. Joy didn't replace my sorrow; it grew beside it. And somehow, that joy became stronger, more rooted, because it was birthed in brokenness.

Try this: name one good thing that bloomed out of your hardest season. One act of kindness. One moment of closeness with God. Write it down. Gratitude doesn't ignore pain—it honors what God can grow in the middle of it.

That's the miracle, isn't it? That God doesn't wait for us to be whole to give us joy. He meets us in the mess, not just the miracle.

---

35 Guthrie, Nancy. *The One Year Book of Hope.* Tyndale House Publishers, 2005.

He brings joy to us in our ashes. He plants it right in the cracks of our story and waters it with His grace. And just like that—through the steady presence of His Word, through the faith of others who have gone before, and through the quiet ministry of the Holy Spirit—joy rises.

Not because everything is fixed. But because *He* is faithful.

God doesn't wait for the fires to cool before He begins His work. He steps into the ashes with us. And from the very place that felt like loss, He grows joy, restores trust, and invites us to believe again. That's the miracle. That's the promise. ***Even the ashes bloom.***

Beauty in BLOOM

Maybe you've been waiting for your story to feel whole again before you believe joy is possible. But here's the truth: God plants joy in broken soil. You don't have to be fully healed to bloom. You just have to be willing to let Him begin.

B–Believe It

- God never wastes our pain.
- Like the redwoods, what looked like devastation may have been preparation.
- Your value isn't measured by what you couldn't hold together. It's anchored in the One who still holds you now.

L–Linger

- Read Romans 5:3–5.
- "*We also glory in our sufferings…*" It feels like a paradox. But linger with this truth: every part of the process—suffering, perseverance, character, hope—is a sacred step in God's refining work. Don't rush past the pain. Sit with it. Let the Holy Spirit meet you there. In the stillness, grace begins to grow. Let these verses become more than words. Let them be an invitation to abide in the transforming presence of God.

O–Observe

- Think back on a time when your life felt scorched: a time of trial, heartbreak, or loss.
- What came from that season that couldn't have been born any other way?
- How has God shown up for you in the middle of the ashes?
- Where in your life do you see new beauty emerging?

- Observe with holy curiosity. The roots may run deeper than you think.

O–Offer Prayer

- Thank God for the redemptive work He has done and the seeds He's still planting.

- Ask for the courage to trust Him, even when the smoke hasn't cleared.

- Pray for eyes to recognize the beauty already beginning to rise.

- Invite the Spirit to continue refining your faith, building your perseverance, and growing your hope.

M–Magnify

- Write a letter to your former self–standing in the ruins, holding shattered dreams, unsure of the next breath. What would you say to her now, knowing what you know? Tell her she won't stay in the ashes forever. Tell her God is already working, already weaving redemption into the very thing she thought would break her.

- Thank God for the ways He has worked through your trials to bring beauty, renewal, and hope. Pray for continued growth in faith and perseverance, trusting that He is always working for your good, even in the most difficult of circumstances.

10

Cultivating Beauty
Reframing the Story,
Reclaiming the Beauty

"There are flowers everywhere for those who want to see them."
—Henri Matisse[36]

Finding the Flowers: A Mindset Shift

In his final years, the French painter Henri Matisse was bound to a wheelchair. Yet his studio blossomed with joy. From his bed, he crafted radiant paper cut-outs: scarlet fronds, cobalt leaves, citrine petals. Art critics often refer to this later stage of Matisse's work as his "second life," marked by joy and resilience. It's as if Matisse took scissors to his suffering and, through grace, reshaped it into praise.

His art whispers a spiritual truth: fire-scorched seasons do not cancel color—they concentrate it.

---

36 Matisse, Henri. *Jazz.* Translated by Sophie Hawkes, George Braziller, 1996, plate 17.

"There are flowers everywhere for those who want to see them," Matisse once said. His words echo Jesus' invitation, "...seek and you will find..." (Matthew 7:7, NIV). Beauty doesn't simply appear; it must be pursued with eyes wide open and hearts attuned to God's goodness. Even in the ashes, God plants blossoms of grace.

This isn't just artistic insight; it's biblical reality. Think of Hagar, wandering in the wilderness after being cast out. Her eyes were clouded with despair until God opened them to see a well of water nearby (Genesis 21:19). Provision was already there. She just needed the spiritual vision to recognize it. Or consider the prophet Elijah, who collapsed under a broom tree, weary and wishing for death. God didn't rebuke him. He gently nourished him with food, rest, and presence, restoring his strength and calling (1 Kings 19). In both stories, beauty was quietly blooming, even in broken places.

Some of Matisse's most joyful "blooms" appeared during his most limited, painful season—proof that creativity, like faith, often flowers not after hardship, but in the midst of it. God doesn't wait until we're whole to work through us. He brings life in the wilderness and rivers in the desert (Isaiah 43:19).

Consider Matisse's *The Open Window* (1905), for example. Sunlight dances across the canvas as bright geraniums spill from a little balcony in Collioure, France. The whole scene seems to hold its breath, as though something beautiful is just about to unfold. In that moment, Matisse doesn't just paint a view; he frames hope itself. In the same way, faith gives us a clearer view through the haze of pain, helping us see the ways God is already bringing beauty back into our lives.

So if you're walking through a season of loss or limitation, take heart: God's palette is not confined to bright days. He creates with shadow as well as light. And sometimes, it's in the quiet aftermath—when everything else feels stripped away—that His most unexpected beauty begins to take shape.

From Ashes to Awareness

There was a time in my life—let's just call it my first marriage—when I walked around with spiritual tunnel vision. And on the days I wasn't looking through a narrow lens, it felt like someone had slipped a blindfold over my eyes.

The way I viewed my role as a wife and woman was shaped by a mix of influences: church teachings, books I read, and well-meaning mentors with firm opinions on "biblical" womanhood. The message that kept surfacing was *submission*. I believed that, as a godly woman, I was supposed to serve my husband and family joyfully, sacrificially, and without question. He would lead; I would follow. He would decide; I would support. I internalized it all—not because someone forced it on me, but because I had gathered fragments of theology, patched them together, and called it truth.

Looking back, I can see how I mistook compliance for humility. I thought I was being faithful. But beneath all the performing and pleasing was a woman crushed by shame, exhausted by striving, and unsure if this was really God's design. I kept asking myself, *Is this what God intended for marriage? For me?*

Spoiler alert: it wasn't.

God didn't just restore my life after everything fell apart. He restored my vision. It was layered and gradual. God gently and patiently peeled back years of distortion. Through single motherhood, heartbreak, financial strain, and divine provision, He showed me what grace really looks like. What freedom in Christ actually means. And perhaps most tenderly, He taught me how to look for beauty again.

That's why the *Looking for Lovely* study by Annie F. Downs hit me so deeply. It came during a season when I was learning how to open my eyes again—not just to God's goodness, but to the redemptive loveliness threaded through my ordinary, imperfect life.

I still remember cracking open the book with a weary but willing heart. I wasn't even sure what I was hoping to find, but I knew I needed more than survival. I needed renewal. In that season, loveliness wasn't obvious. My life felt more like a pile of pieces than a picture of peace. But through each session, God invited me to shift my perspective—not by pretending the hard things didn't happen, but by noticing how He was still working in the middle of them.

Downs's words echoed what God was already whispering to my spirit: *Look again. There's beauty here, too.* Whether it was the kindness of a friend, a sunset on a lonely evening, or the slow rebuilding of hope, I started paying attention. And the more I looked, the more I saw.

Downs wrote, "I want us to learn to look for the lovely all around us and collect it, hold it close, and see how God drops beautiful things into our lives at just the right time to help us step forward on our own paths."[37] That truth gripped me. I wasn't just learning to see beauty; I was learning to *gather* it. To carry it with me as proof that God hadn't abandoned me in the ashes. He was planting something even there.

That Bible study wasn't just another devotional. It was a turning point. A spiritual reorientation. A reminder that loveliness isn't loud, but it's always present for those with eyes to see. And

---

37 Downs, Annie F. *Looking for Lovely: Collecting the Moments That Matter.* B&H Publishing Group, 2016.

after so many years of walking blind, I was finally learning how to look again. "Open my eyes to see the wonderful truths in your instructions" (Psalm 119:18, NLT).

God wasn't just changing my circumstances. He was changing *me*. Teaching me to see with wonder again. Showing me that *seeing beauty* isn't just a personality trait or artistic gift—it's a spiritual practice. A form of faith.

Learning to look for beauty was just the beginning. As God opened my eyes, He also began to stir something deeper: a desire not only to notice beauty but to nurture it. To move from passive appreciation to intentional cultivation. Beauty, I realized, isn't just something we stumble upon—it's something we participate in. And often, it's the smallest acts of noticing that begin to prepare the soil of our hearts for something lovely to grow.

Collecting and Cultivating Beauty

As I mentioned before, my oldest son is a bit of an art connoisseur. He's taught me more about brushstrokes and backstories than I ever learned in school, and he's helped me develop a greater appreciation for beauty, both on canvas and in life. Our shared viewings—from Da Vinci's *Mona Lisa* and Rembrandt's *Night Watch* to Van Gogh's *Sunflowers* and Degas's *Little Dancer Aged Fourteen*—have become cherished moments together. A rhythm of slowing down, standing still, and noticing what others might pass by.

But of all the art we've seen, nothing impacted me quite like our visit to Musée de l'Orangerie in Paris, where we viewed Claude Monet's full-size, original *Water Lilies*. I had always assumed the smaller framed pieces I'd seen in museums were the whole picture. But stepping into the two large, oval-shaped rooms that house his eight massive panels of lilies and light—each one spanning over

40 feet long and nearly 7 feet high—I realized how much of the masterpiece I had been missing.

I stood there in awe, completely surrounded by color—lavender shadows, rippling water, blossoms that seemed to float between heaven and earth. And I couldn't help but think: *How often do we live our lives only seeing a cropped version of what God is doing?*

When we're walking through sorrow or shame, it's easy to develop tunnel vision. Pain narrows our focus. We fixate on the cracks, the losses, the mess right in front of us, and miss the masterpiece being painted just beyond the frame.

I'd spent years seeing only fragments of my story. But standing there, fully immersed in Monet's sweeping vision, I felt God whisper, *There's more. Lift your eyes. The full picture is coming into view.*

Monet did not just paint beauty. He *cultivated* it.

He was as much a gardener as he was an artist, lovingly tending the grounds at Giverny, where many of his floral subjects grew. He even helped design the gallery space, carefully considering how viewers would be immersed in the quiet elegance of his lilies and light.

Monet is often quoted as saying, "My garden is my most beautiful masterpiece."[38] He knew what we're all learning: gardens don't grow by accident, and neither does beauty. It's curated. It's cultivated. It's intentional.

Just like Monet carefully arranged each bloom before lifting his brush to canvas, we're invited to tend to the soil of our hearts, making space for the lovely to take root.

---

[38] Commonly attributed to Claude Monet, though no verifiable primary source has been identified. See "Claude Monet Artist Overview and Analysis," *The Art Story*, www.theartstory.org/artist/monet-claude/.

Beauty doesn't usually arrive like a ready-made bouquet from heaven. It's something we learn to see. And then, it's something we learn to grow.

What we nurture matters. What we notice grows. And when we begin collecting beauty—like petals of grace scattered through our ordinary days—we partner with God in His creative, redemptive work.

Practical Rhythms for Cultivating Beauty

If beauty doesn't just appear but must be looked for and cultivated, then how do we begin? How do we train our eyes and hearts to recognize the lovely, especially in seasons that feel anything but?

We begin with intention.

Cultivating beauty is less about adding more to your to-do list and more about slowing down enough to notice what's already there. One of the practices I've adopted is my *Joy Jar*. It's as simple as it sounds: a jar, some slips of paper, and the quiet discipline of paying attention. Each day, I write down one thing that brought me joy, made me smile, or helped me sense God's nearness. Some days it's deep and sacred—an answered prayer, a moment of connection with my sons, a verse that met me in my mess. Other days it's something light and fleeting—a really good cup of coffee, a song I'd forgotten I loved, sunlight through the kitchen window.

When gathered, these tiny moments become something weighty—proof that even when life feels uncertain or heavy, God is still scattering beauty across the path.

Another rhythm is offering *prayers of gratitude*, not just for the obvious gifts but for the small ones—the ones we'd miss if we weren't looking. Gratitude doesn't deny grief or gloss over pain; it simply says, "Even here, God is good." When we begin our days with thankfulness, it tills the soil of our hearts and makes room for joy to grow.

And then, there's the practice of *noticing the lovely*. This takes practice, especially when your soul feels weary. But when we start looking—truly looking—we realize how much beauty God has already placed around us: in nature, in people, in Scripture, in unexpected moments of peace.

Here's the truth: beauty is not accidental. It's intentional. Just like gardens must be planted and nourished, the same is true of joy, gratitude, and wonder. We won't stumble into lives marked by loveliness; we cultivate them, one small act of noticing at a time.

So today, begin with one step. Write down one joy. Say one prayer of thanks. Look for one thing that reflects God's beauty. It may feel small, but you are planting something sacred.

And here's what I've found again and again: when we intentionally look for beauty, we begin to notice it more. But when we *invite God* into that process through prayer, we begin to see beauty not just around us, but *within* us.

Prayer is one of the most powerful ways God reshapes our vision. Not because it fixes everything, but because it *changes how we see* everything. In prayer, I've discovered that beauty isn't always bold or obvious. Sometimes, it's a shift in mindset, a softened heart, a deeper breath in the middle of the chaos. Prayer has been the place where my perspective changed, where gratitude was built brick by brick, and where I learned to sit in God's presence, not just bring Him my petitions.

Prayer is not a transaction; it's a transformation. It's where I've seen God highlight what I would have missed: the hidden loveliness in a weary day, the unexpected grace in a difficult conversation, the reminder that I am not alone. It's in prayer that God often opens my eyes to His beauty, His nearness, His goodness. It's also in prayer where I've begun to see beauty in myself again. Not because of anything I've earned or perfected, but because when I'm still enough to listen, I hear the gentle truth: *You are My beloved. I am still at work in you.*

Prayer creates space. Space to see. Space to breathe. Space to bloom.

So when you don't know where to begin, start here. Sit with God. Say the honest thing. Notice what He brings to the surface. And let your eyes begin to adjust to the light of His presence.

Your prayers, your Joy Jar, your daily rhythms of gratitude—these are your seeds. They may feel small or hidden, but they are part of the masterpiece God is growing in and through you.

Music and the Masterpiece

As I began to look for and discover beauty around me, I also began to see beauty within myself for the first time in a long time.

Years of hearing my inner critic shout at the top of its lungs, *"You are not enough. You aren't worthy of respect. You aren't worthy of love. You deserve this pain,"* took time to unravel and release. As I listened to the song "Anyway" by Nichole Nordeman, I was reminded that God sees us as beautiful, even as we sit covered in ash, even in the midst of our shame.

At the time I was going through my divorce, Christy Nockels, a well-known Christian music artist and worship leader, was on part-time staff at our church and led worship periodically. Hearing her belt out "Marvelous Light" as the congregation sang in unison with her nearly brought me to my knees…every time.

This song became my declaration. A turning point. Each time the chorus rose, I felt my spirit do the same. There was this imagery of running—*running* out of darkness, out of shame, and straight into the brilliance of God's presence. It echoed the truth of 1 Peter 2:9: that I was no longer defined by my past, but by the One who had called me His own. His light didn't just expose the broken places; it healed them. It didn't humiliate me; it held me. Shame had told me to hide. But in those moments of worship, I sensed God inviting me into His light—not to be exposed, but to be restored. To finally believe that I wasn't just someone worth saving. I was someone worth loving.

Because that's what His light does. It doesn't come to shame you, but to *restore* you. It brings truth that gently untangles the lies. It doesn't spotlight your wounds to wound you again. It illuminates your worth so you can finally see yourself the way He does. His light allows you to recognize the beauty He's been cultivating in you all along—the masterpiece He never stopped shaping, even in the shadows.

Standing in church surrounded by voices singing, I realized something: I wasn't just part of the crowd worshiping the Creator. *I was His creation*—a melody He composed on purpose. A masterpiece still becoming. The light didn't just shine on me; it sang over me. And in the presence of that kind of love, shame didn't stand a chance.

In his letter to the Ephesians, Paul puts it plainly: "For we are God's handiwork, created in Christ Jesus to do good works, which God prepared in advance for us to do" (Ephesians 2:10, NIV).

You are His handiwork—His masterpiece. Not an accident. Not a backup plan. Not a fixer-upper. A one-of-a-kind creation, crafted with intention, beauty, and purpose. And like any great artist, God didn't leave anything to chance. Every strength, every story, even the places you've seen as weaknesses—He's using them all in His redemptive design.

I think about this every time I walk through an art gallery. As we pause in front of each piece, my son often notices details I'd miss on my own—brush strokes, technique, contrast, depth. The more I learn to see through his eyes, the more I appreciate the variety and uniqueness of each work.

And that's exactly what happens when we begin to see ourselves through *God's* eyes. We begin to understand our true worth. Not because we've earned it, but because we've been *named* it. Chosen. Loved. Redeemed. Enough.

He is still writing your story in strokes of beauty, grace, and purpose. You are not a forgotten sketch in the corner of His studio. You are His ongoing masterpiece. Every chapter, even the painful ones, is being redeemed with intentionality.

And here's the truth I'm learning: beauty isn't a reward for getting it all right. It's a *reflection*. A reflection of God's love. Of His presence. Of His transforming work in you. The more we step into His marvelous light, the more clearly we begin to see it—not just around us, but *within* us.

God has been cultivating beauty within you all along.

Not just in spite of the ashes, but because of them.

And now, with the light of His truth shining on your story, you have the chance to see what He's been shaping:

A life touched by grace.

A heart still capable of blooming.
A masterpiece in the making.
So keep showing up.
Keep tending the soil.
Keep choosing the light.

Because cultivating beauty isn't about perfection, it's about participation. It's about letting the Artist have His way, even when you can't yet see the whole picture. And as you do, may you discover this:

The beauty you've been looking for?

It's been growing in you all along.

Beauty in BLOOM

B–Believe It

- Beauty is a choice. Not always of circumstance, but of perspective.
- Gratitude cultivates joy. And joy invites beauty to grow.
- God is still painting your story, even from the charred pages.
- Suffering doesn't get the final word. God does, and His word is always redemption.

L–Linger

- "Finally, brothers and sisters, whatever is true, whatever is noble, whatever is right, whatever is pure, whatever is lovely, whatever is admirable—if anything is excellent or praiseworthy—think about such things" (Philippians 4:8, NIV).

O–Observe

- What are some small, intentional ways you can create or notice more beauty in:
  - Your home?
  - Your schedule?
  - Your mindset?
  - Your relationships?
- What habits help you practice gratitude and joy daily?
- How has your understanding of beauty shifted in this season of your life?

O–Offer Prayer

Lord,
Sometimes beauty feels hidden—
lost beneath the ashes of worry and weariness.

But I believe You are still here,
inviting me to see through Your eyes.
Help me notice what is lovely,
even in the quiet and the undone places.
Shift my focus from what's broken
to what You are restoring.
Thank You for the small graces—
sunrises, kind words, deep breaths, and new beginnings.
Even when I can't see it clearly,
remind me that You are growing beauty in me.
Let today be a fresh start.
Open my heart to wonder.
Lead me back to You through beauty.
In Jesus' name, Amen.

M–Magnify

Choose one (or more) of the following as a spiritual practice:

- Gratitude Journal: Write three things each day you're thankful for, especially the small or unexpected.
- Redemption Collage: Use images, words, and Bible verses to create a visual reminder of how God has brought beauty from your ashes.
- Make a Joy Jar: Write down one lovely thing each day—a kind word, a moment of laughter, a sunset—and place it in the jar. Revisit these on hard days.
- 30-Day Beauty Hunt: Commit to writing one beautiful thing each day for a month. Even one sentence counts. Just open your eyes and your heart.

Conclusion

If you've made it to this page, pause and take a deep breath—not because this journey is over, but because you've done something sacred. You showed up. You faced hard and holy things. You leaned in, listened for God's voice, and made space for your healing. That is no small thing.

You've walked through grief and grace, silence and surrender—through beauty that bloomed where you never expected. Maybe healing didn't look the way you imagined. But here you are: still tender. Still standing. Still held.

Thank you for trusting me with your time, your questions, and maybe even your pain.

But more than that, thank you for believing that God could meet you here: in the in-between, in the broken places, in the parts still being mended.

Healing doesn't mean you're "over it." Sometimes, it's learning to live honestly with what still aches. Sometimes, it's releasing what you buried long ago. Sometimes, it's simply being still long enough to notice—*you are already in bloom.*

You don't need a perfect ending to witness God's goodness. You don't need a tidy resolution to know you're growing. Beauty isn't something far off in the distance. It's rising here, now, even in places that once felt ruined.

Even changed ground is still good ground in the hands of God.

God has never asked you to bloom alone.

He tends the soil. He waters the roots.

And yes—He is doing a new thing: "See, I am doing a new thing! Now it springs up; do you not perceive it? I am making a way in the wilderness and streams in the wasteland" (Isaiah 43:19, NIV).

If all you've done is keep showing up—keep surrendering, keep trusting, keep whispering yes through the tears—that is more than enough.

So keep going, even if the steps are small. Watch for beauty in unexpected places. Offer yourself grace when it feels like you're stuck. And if you're still in the messy middle, let me be the one to whisper what I hope you'll come to believe:

God is in your story. Still. Always.

Maybe you still wonder: *What if healing never fully comes this side of heaven?* Here's what I hope you'll remember: God's promise isn't that we'll never ache again, but that we'll never walk through it alone. His presence is the healing.

Even when full restoration feels far off, you are still being renewed, still being shaped, still being held. Some healing takes a lifetime. Some won't fully unfold until eternity. But even now, in the waiting and the wondering, there is hope.

There is beauty.

There is Jesus.

"God never hurries. There are no deadlines against which He must work.
Only to know this is to quiet our spirits and relax our nerves."
—*A. W. Tozer*[39]

So take a breath. God is not in a rush with your heart. He is patient and gentle, working below the surface in ways you cannot yet see.

And when you question whether beauty can really come from this, lean into the promise:

> *To all who mourn in Israel,*
> *He will give a crown of beauty for ashes,*
> *a joyous instead of mourning,*
> *festive praise instead of despair.*
> *In their righteousness, they will be like great oaks*
> *that the Lord has planted for His own glory.*
> *(Isaiah 61:3, NLT)*

You are not a lost cause. You are His planting, and He is faithful to tend what He plants.

If you've been walking a long road, tired of trying, aching for change—take heart.

As Galatians 6:9 (NIV) reminds us: "Let us not grow weary in doing good, for at the proper time we will reap a harvest if we do not give up."

So keep surrendering. Keep believing.

You are living proof that even the ashes bloom.

* * *

---

39 Tozer, A. W. *The Pursuit of God.* Christian Publications, 1948.

A Prayer as You Go

Lord, thank You for healing the broken places in my heart.
As I walk forward, help me to embrace the beauty You are
creating in me.
I trust You with my past, my present, and my future.
Help me to walk in the truth that I am already in bloom—
not by my own strength, but by Your grace.
In Jesus' name, Amen.

*   *   *

A Blessing for the Path Ahead

May you trust that the breaking was not wasted.
May you see the beauty quietly blooming beneath the surface.
May you walk forward—not with all the answers,
but with the assurance that the One who planted hope in you
will be faithful to bring it to full bloom.

You may not know all the next steps.
I don't know all the details of your story.
But I know the One who does.
And I believe He's still writing something beautiful.

You've walked bravely. You've let light in.
And now, as you turn this final page, I hope you know:
You are not alone. You are not forgotten.
And even now—especially now—you are blooming.

I'm cheering you on. I'm praying for you.
And I'm so grateful you chose to walk this path with me.
May your heart be encouraged to know:
Even the ashes bloom.

www.ingramcontent.com/pod-product-compliance
Lightning Source LLC
Chambersburg PA
CBHW020247130626
46549CB00005B/2099